...My God Story

C O N T E N T S

F O R E W O R D

Have you ever met someone and just felt that instant "connection"?

I have. It's a wonderful feeling to know that you "connect" with someone. You have a common background, common traits, or common experience - and you click. It is as if you have known this person your whole life. This kind of "connection" forms an instant bond, and many times you find encouragement or glean pertinent help from the encounter.

Meeting God works the same way.

Many of us have a certain "God Story" - that memorable moment when we met God and our lives changed direction.

That is what this book is about. It details REAL people's lives and their REAL encounters with a God who loves them. Many of the stories are dramatic, like the guy who worked for a famous crime family, while other stories document the regular "Joe," like the couple who got divorced because of the everyday trials and stresses of life.

Where are you today in your life? Are you happy, successful, and thriving on the outside, but feeling something far different on the inside? Or are you really struggling with this thing called "life"? Maybe you are tired of dealing with fear, insecurity, and inferiority. Maybe you are just tired of all the pressure and stress of making a living or trying to be a good mom or dad. Or perhaps you are dreading life itself, even thinking about suicide because it seems like the only option left.

Is there something in your life you regret?

Is there something in your life you need to accept?

Are you afraid?

I encourage you to read the following stories. Perhaps you will make a "connection" with at least one of these people, if not more. I pray that you will see the joy that arises out of the despair, the beauty that arises out of the ashes, and that when we connect with God, we are forever changed.

It is my hope that you will meet God through these stories, but most of all, I pray that you will meet Him in the midst of your own life experience.

And no matter what your situation in life is, I can assure you that God wants to MEET YOU!

Pastor Bob
Calvary Chapel Fort Lauderdale, Florida

...My God Story

one

B O B ' S   S T O R Y

An Unlikely Choice

I was set on being a millionaire by the age of twenty-one. In high school I looked forward to the future with high aspirations, great expectations, and immense goals. Always a social person, I had the ability to blend in with any type of crowd. Grunge, hippie, greasy, preppie, or trendy - I became them all. Yet, despite all my lofty ideals, plans, and abilities, I often wondered who I was.

As a young person, I was totally into music. You could ask me about any band or song title, and I would know who played what song and on what album. I worked my way up the ranks at a local music store and then got a job as a buyer. My boss soon realized that I had a knack for picking a hit record. But he wasn't the only one who discovered my "talent."

One day I received a call from Capitol Records, and before long I was working with one of the top recording labels in the country, helping them push the hits and enjoying my new status as a record rep.

"How you doing? I'm Bob Coy, Capitol Records," I would typically say as I extended my hand with my impressive looking business card. Along with the impressive job came the outwardly impressive lifestyle. I had the sports car, the drugs, the girls, and the excitement - all at the age of twenty-one. I looked very impressive, but only outwardly.

Inwardly, I was learning the hard reality that success usually comes with a high price tag. In my case, losing myself in the drug culture was how I spent my success. Cocaine and other "party" drugs turned into a regular lifestyle for me. I thought I could handle the drugs, but I soon learned that the drugs were handling me instead.

After repeated warnings from my boss, I tried to quit drinking and doing drugs so I wouldn't lose my job, but what my boss didn't know was that there was an even greater problem threatening my job status.

I had agoraphobia, an abnormal fear of open or public places or social settings. Here I was a big time rep with a major recording company, seemingly extroverted and "together" on the outside, but on the inside I was suffering from so much fear that I would break out in panic attacks. I specifically remember having one attack while I was in a company meeting at Capitol Records. After it happened, I never wanted to go to another meeting because it would remind me of the attack. Another time I had a panic attack in a department store while I was with an artist at an in-store appearance, so, of course, I never wanted to walk into a department store again. My phobia was so dreadful that I actually stayed in my apartment for more than a month once because I was too afraid to venture out and be around people.

Have you ever experienced that type of fear? It is a serious bondage. It virtually paralyzes you from being able to function normally. Because of the fear, I started calling in to the company to get out of meetings and appointments. Eventually I lost my job.

Those who struggle with panic also tend to battle insecurity. I had succeeded, but had an underlying feeling that I wasn't worthy to be in the position that I was in. Deep down I was still trying to find out who I was. In a way, I was like a chameleon. I let everyone else determine my likes and dislikes. If you liked something, then I liked it. I wanted to fit in. I guess you could say I was also like a golden retriever! I liked everybody, and I wanted everybody to like me.

When you are trying to please everybody, you end up losing yourself in the process. The secret to failure is trying to please everyone. You can't define your own identity because you've taken on the identity of whoever it is you are around at the time that you're trying to impress.

So many of us struggle with the same questions: Who am I? Why am I here? What is my purpose? In all of my partying, in all of my promiscuity, and in all of my seeking after success, I was looking for answers and acceptance, and I would do just about anything to be accepted.

But then something happened. I met God.

This doped-up, fearful, and accommodating guy met God in the midst of a flurry of sins, weaknesses, and trials. I had become a "party animal" record industry junkie, a hardcore, demanding entertainment director, and an irresponsible husband to a woman I was married to for only three weeks. Yet, in the thick of a broken-down life, I discovered that God loved ME and accepted ME just the way I was. I learned that I had an identity in Jesus Christ, I had a purpose for my life, and I no longer needed to be in bondage to my fears because God was in control of my life.

As I began to trust God, my fears decreased. After all, most of my fears were not grounded in reality. When you find God, you discover that HIS TRUTH is reality.

When I first came to Christ I regretted my failure in the record industry. I used to think, "God, if You had given me Your Spirit while I was working for Capitol Records, I could have really been used by You there." Now I realize that everything happened just the way it was supposed to in order for me to fully surrender the life I was living to the life that God wanted and planned for me. The things that I did or the choices I made did not surprise the Lord. God is sovereign. He knew my every thought and used even my sins and bad choices to bring me to the place where I was ready to meet Him!

I left the entertainment industry in Las Vegas. I was broke but happy! Off drugs and alcohol, the Lord had turned my life around and was giving me new desires, especially the desire to serve Him full-time in ministry. In just a short time I was offered a job at Calvary Chapel in Las Vegas. Making only $300 per month and driving an old '65 Chevy, I was living on cloud nine! Shortly after taking the job, the senior pastor asked me to start participating in the service by speaking and making announcements. My fear started to rear its head again, but after much prayer, I was able to speak publicly.

It took six years, but God finally answered my prayer for a wife. Diane loved the Lord and desired to serve Him. When we got married, I felt my life was complete.

Eventually the Lord put it on my heart to start a church in Fort Lauderdale, Florida, and I've been here serving Him ever since. I actually speak to thousands of people on a weekly basis with cameras rolling and all. Sometimes I still can't believe it myself. I would consider myself an unlikely choice, but God didn't. He gives life to the dead and calls things that are not as though they were (Romans 4:17).

What the Lord did for me, He can do for you.

"...being confident of this very thing, that He
who has begun a good work in you
will complete it until the day of Jesus Christ."
Philippians 1:6

GREG'S STORY

Glitz, Glamour, and Girls

"I was stunned. I hung up the phone, and all I could do was pace back and forth across the room. My emotions jumbled together while my thoughts raced wildly around in my head. 'How could this have happened?'"

Life was pretty good. I was moving and shaking in a five-star world most people my age only dream about. Money. Travel. Parties. Privilege. And beautiful people. I was climbing the ladder of success as one of the top fashion models in the world. My friends were fun and famous, and I was having the time of my life.

Modeling was not my life's objective; I more or less stumbled into it. In my last year of college, I began dating a beautiful local model. While attending one of her photo shoots, I was approached by an agent who asked if I would be interested in modeling. Before long, I found myself in New York City working with the Ford Agency, one of the top modeling agencies. The next thing I knew, I was told I was going to Paris to work!

Paris was wild, exciting, and fast. In no time I got caught up in the culture of the fashion world. I was soon living a lifestyle completely contrary to the one I grew up in. I was earning lots of money, traveling the world, and dating a steady stream of gorgeous women.

After two years, I moved back to the United States. I began traveling between New York and Miami Beach where a good friend and I had invested in a nightclub.

Miami's hot summer nights, lush tropical landscape, and capricious atmosphere were the perfect backdrop for our new club, and it wasn't long before "The Whiskey" became a popular hot spot. However, behind all the glamour and fast living there was this persistent nagging thought. I knew my high maintenance lifestyle was going to catch up with me. I grew up in a God-fearing home, and though I had blown God off, so to speak, I knew deep down I wasn't living the way I should.

One night, as I opened the door to my hotel room, I noticed the red message light blinking. I grabbed a cold beer out of the mini-bar before pushing the button to retrieve my voice mail. The message was from my friend in New York. His voice sounded frantic, so I immediately called him back. "Hello?" he answered. When he heard my voice, he didn't beat around the bush, but told me straight up that my former girlfriend had just died of AIDS.

I was stunned. I hung up the phone, and all I could do was pace back and forth across the room. My emotions jumbled together while my thoughts raced wildly around in my head. "How could this have happened?" I thought. "How?" Nicole was so beautiful and healthy looking. I had never even seen her sniffle.

Fear and dread became my constant companions. The well-meaning attempts of friends slapping me on the back trying to comfort and reassure me that "everything is going to be okay" did not bring me even a flicker of hope.

I remember feeling an intense fear. I had been told that my former girlfriend had died of AIDS, and I didn't know whether I had it or not. I didn't know what to do or where to go. It was all so overwhelming. I knew I needed to be tested, but I was embarrassed and didn't want to go to a place where I would be recognized. So I drove to another town to take the test.

The people at the clinic said it would take about a week and a half before they would have the results. It was a long, agonizing wait. I kept modeling and wearing a plastic smile, but my emotions were all over the place and my mind was racing so much I couldn't sleep.

During the waiting period, I worried constantly about what was going to happen to me. Everything I thought mattered all of a sudden seemed trivial and useless. By the time I drove back to the clinic a week later, I was hanging on by only a thread of hope that this would all go away, but if the results showed that I was not carrying the HIV virus, boy did I plan to party hard! The only "reformation" in my thinking was that now I knew I needed to be more responsible in my sexual exploits.

I walked in the clinic, sat down, and looked at the piece of paper the nurse gave me. It read, "FOR THOSE WHO HAVE TESTED POSITIVE FOR THE HIV VIRUS." When I asked the nurse about it, she matter-of-factly told me that I was HIV positive. As the tears burned my eyes, she patted my arm with her hand with an attitude of "I feel sorry for you, but this is as close as I can get."

All of a sudden I had a major disease that no one really knew much about, except that it was an impending death sentence. The things that had once served as my primary focus (career, money, parties, women) were now meaningless. I was devastated. Again, I tried to share my fears with my friends, but their words of encouragement felt like cheap advice that makes you feel worse after hearing it. They just couldn't understand the anguish I was facing.

Then there was the anger. I was angry at my former girlfriend and with myself. I was angry that I would never be able to get married or have children. I also agonized over the humiliation that this knowledge would bring my parents. Their lives would never be normal again, and the shame and stigma of having a son with this disease would be so hard on them.

A few days later, I was in my hotel room with my friend who had flown in from New York to spend some time with me. We looked at each other and started to cry. I said to him, "I don't want to die." "Hey, man, I don't want you to die either," he answered in a choked voice.

There didn't seem to be any way out. I felt lost, scared, hurt, and desperate. Then I started searching for answers, not just answers to this disease, but also answers to life. One Sunday morning, I turned on the television. Flipping through the channels, I came upon a church service. I stopped and watched. I found myself thinking that I really should try going to church. I remembered that I had just given a friend of mine who goes to church some drink coupons and a promotional shirt from my club. So I called him up and asked him if I could go with him sometime. Needless to say, this was the last thing my friend had expected to hear from me, but he jumped on it.

As we drove up to a warehouse, my anticipation turned to cynicism. People were dressed casually and looked... well, strange - strange for church, that is. The piano player had long hair, the music was upbeat, and everyone was smiling. The whole thing really began to annoy me. Yet, as the music played on, something stirred in my soul. All of a sudden, I began to cry, and I couldn't stop.

God spoke to my heart that day. And the message was clear: He loved me and wanted to meet my deepest need in the midst of this disease and all my pain, fear, shame, and hopelessness. That day, I asked Jesus to come into my heart, convinced that He loved me and would take care of me, no matter what happened next.

Immediately, I felt a huge burden being lifted off my shoulders.

A few days later, I went to my doctor's appointment with a positive attitude and a sense of peace. I told the doctor that I was a Christian now and I was going to trust that God would do what He wanted to do with my life.

God began to transform me. I got out of the bar business and abandoned the party scene. I was looking at life differently and experiencing more joy than I had ever known, even though I was still HIV positive. I was no longer comfortable living the life I had lived before. I exchanged drinking and drugs for Bible reading, praying, and church fellowship, and for the first time in my life I was finally experiencing real joy and happiness.

I told my parents I was HIV positive, and, although they were shocked and grieved, being Christians, they responded with grace and love.

I began to realize that the anger and resentment I felt toward my former girlfriend and her parents for not telling me that she had AIDS was not accomplishing anything. God even helped me to understand the pain and hurt that Nicole's parents felt. Then I found out that they actually thought I knew all along!

One of the most important lessons I learned, and one that helped me to forgive Nicole, was that I was responsible for my own actions. You know, I believe we all have a tendency to go through this life blaming others for our own troubles. We blame other people because we don't want to face the music of our own actions.

Sometimes God rescues us from our own actions, but other times He loves us through the consequences. In my case, God did both.

Today I am married to a beautiful Christian model from South Africa named Ashleigh. Together we have traveled the world modeling and conducting Bible studies for those in the industry. God has richly blessed me. I never even dreamed I would be able to get married, but He brought Ashleigh into my life and has given us the ability to reach out to others and make our lives count for Him.

It has been nine years since I tested positive for the HIV virus, and my future is still uncertain, but, one thing I know for sure, testing HIV positive was the best thing that ever happened to me. I met God in the midst of HIV, and meeting Him changed the course of my life.

> *"Concerning this thing I pleaded with the Lord three times that it*
> *might depart from me. And He said to me, 'My grace is sufficient for*
> *you, for My strength is made perfect in weakness.'*
> *Therefore most gladly I will rather boast in my infirmities, that the power*
> *of Christ may rest upon me. Therefore I take pleasure in infirmities,*
> *in reproaches, in needs, in persecutions, in distresses, for Christ's sake.*
> *For when I am weak, then I am strong."*
> *2 Corinthians 12:8-10*

THINK ABOUT THIS

We read Greg's story and hear him say that testing HIV positive was the best thing that ever happened to him. It's hard to imagine those same words coming out of our mouth, and yet, we've each had our own set of painful circumstances invade our lives and change us for the better.

The easy thing to do at those times is to be angry, bitter, and in constant fear, but the Bible says that if we turn to God in our suffering, He will give us a peace that is beyond comprehension. It's the only explanation for Greg's attitude. It's beyond human understanding.

Allow God to take those painful circumstances in your life and use them to make your life better. It will be a challenge, but with God on your side, it's a challenge worth taking.

QUESTIONS WE SHOULD ASK

Do you have any habits in your life that could lead to a painful outcome?

What is it in your life that creates intense fear?

Why does the idea of surrendering one's life to God seem so difficult?

Appendix...

Bad Habits, Fear, Assurance of Salvation

three

H A N K ' S   S T O R Y

A Marriage or a Nightmare

*"All our issues rapidly rose to the surface.
We were explosive together and even dangerous at times."*

I grew up in upstate New York. At the age of four, my father abandoned our family. Then, at the age of eleven, my next-door neighbor, a sheriff for a city in the state of New York, molested me.

The devastation of my father's abandonment, coupled with the physical violation by a man I trusted, left me with a deep-seated anger and pessimism that invaded my entire life.

I found alcohol and drugs early on, and they helped me escape the pain. Then, at twelve years old, I met Marty who was a drug dealer and a bookie. To me, Marty's life seemed exciting, fun, and free. The more time I spent around him, the more influenced I was by him, and soon I was doing drugs everyday.

A few years later my family moved to Florida, and my mother

divorced for the second time. A couple of years after that I dropped out of high school in the middle of my senior year and ran away from home.

I was always mad at something. I hated everyone, including myself. I was especially angry with my father for leaving and Sheriff Roy for molesting me. I was a time bomb ready to explode.

I met Anita at a point in my life when I was desperately craving someone's love and attention. We got married right away, but our marriage was in trouble from the start. I wore a lot of masks and always needed her approval and acceptance. There were many volatile moments in our marriage, including some acts of abuse on my part. When our first child was born, we split up.

After our divorce, I tried to get my life together and get off drugs, but I kept relapsing. Finally I hit my bottom. I committed to getting clean and staying clean. I went to Narcotics Anonymous and worked their recovery program.

About a year later I met some friends who invited me to church. As I sat in the service, I was struck by something the pastor said: "Jesus is the Jewish Messiah." I thought, "Okay, I'm in the right place!" I was raised Jewish and had been through my bar mitzvah at thirteen.

I really enjoyed the church and the people. There was a love and a peace and a unity that I had never seen before. The pastor gave an invitation, and I went forward to give my life to Jesus Christ.

I started reading the Bible, and God began to teach me through it. Soon those parts of my life that I had buried under anger and pessimism were exposed. I had to take a hard look at the issues that had caused them.

I met Diana at the church. Like me, she also had always needed the approval of others. At eighteen, she married a wealthy guy who gave her all the material things she could ever want. They moved to Colombia, where their relationship became rocky, so she divorced him and moved back to the States. But Diana had gotten used to the affluent lifestyle and didn't want to give it up, so she got a job as a dancer in a strip club.

Night after night she watched married men come into the club seeking sexual favors. It did a lot to reinforce her distrust of men. After six years, she stopped dancing, but her need for men to approve of her never left.

Diana and I started dating right away. In three weeks we were engaged. Four months after that, we got married. It was a real rush. But our life together was anything but blissful. All our issues rapidly rose to the surface. We were explosive together and even dangerous at times.

There was a lot of verbal abuse and domination. Our fights escalated to the point where I would hit Diana in my rage. Finally, she decided that if I hit her one more time, she was going to call the police. I did hit her again, and I went to jail. But it didn't break me. I remember sitting there in the jail stewing over everything that had just happened. I was sure it was Diana's fault, that I hit her because she provoked me. In fact, I told myself that she was selfish and abusive and that nothing I did for her was ever good enough. I never looked at my own part in the violence – I just shifted all the blame onto Diana.

I was released from jail, but nothing changed. We struggled through the next few months. Once again, I became violent, and once again Diana called the cops. I was arrested and thrown in jail for fifteen days for violating my probation.

This time, as I sat in jail, God broke me. I had come to the end of myself, and instead of blaming Diana, God really made me take a look at my own sins. I knew I was wrong. I had finally come to a place of true repentance.

Within a day, I formed a prayer group in jail and started reaching out to other men in the same cellblock.

Diana, too, started seeking God. She separated herself from her friends and put her life in God's hands. Even in the smallest things, she knew that God was telling her to stop seeking the approval of others and be dependent only on Him.

The judge took mercy on my case, my probation was restored, and I was released after thirteen days.

We began the long road to restoration and recovery in our lives and in our fragile marriage. I moved in with one of the pastors from my church for three months. Every day he taught me and counseled me.

God was working in Diana's heart. She came to realize that she could never be a wife to anyone as long as she was ruled by her own insecurities.

God showed both of us that we needed to have our identity in Christ. Neither one of us could take each other's sins personally. We needed to act in love towards one another, not in anger, fear, jealousy, or judgment.

After going through several stages of counseling, the day finally came when I moved back home.

Today Diana and I have a child and lead Bible studies for married couples. We have grown and learned a lot about God, one another, and ourselves. It's not always easy, but we know that God is able to do exceedingly abundantly more than we could ask, think, or imagine because with Him all things are possible.

"Let no one despise your youth, but be an example to the believers in word, in conduct, in love, in spirit, in faith, in purity."
1 Timothy 4:12

THINK ABOUT THIS

Hank's decision to give his life to Christ did not bring about instant change. He and Diana met at church. His life still had a lot of garbage in it when they were married. Sometimes we believe that just by accepting God, or hanging out with those who have accepted God, we will see instant changes in our lives, but change takes time. It would sure be a lot easier if God would just snap His fingers and change our lives, but that doesn't happen.

God wants to see permanent changes in our lives, not temporary ones, and that only happens when we want to make the changes no matter what the cost. First we have to understand why the changes are needed. Then we must come to realize how much better off we'll be once they occur.

God gave us free will, and if we choose to live in sin, even as Christians, we can, but the Bible teaches that our adversary, the devil, walks around like a roaring lion, seeking whom he may devour (1 Peter 5:8). He wants to use sin in our lives to destroy us. But God has a better plan. His plan is to give us a future and a hope.

QUESTIONS WE SHOULD ASK

What sin is making your life worse?

How do you deal with your anger and insecurity?

What is adding frustration to your life, and what changes need to take place?

Appendix . . .

Abuse, Anger, Insecurity, Perseverance

four

C A R R I E ' S   S T O R Y

Robbed of Innocence

*"By now Carrie was in a catatonic state.
And it seemed there was no hope left. I was distraught at their
prognosis and felt agony for my daughter's life."*

I was like so many mothers. I wanted my children to be brought up with good values, love, and a sense of belonging, but my life had been difficult. I was on my second marriage and had four kids to take care of. I loved them all dearly and did my best to provide them with the parenting and support they needed.

We lived in California where we attended a local church. The kids and I took part in many of the church's programs. My children, aged five to thirteen, loved church, and they especially loved the youth pastor. A charismatic, approachable man, he encouraged the children and invested in their spiritual and mental lives.

Things were going well for us until one day I got a call from the senior pastor. He asked me to come down to the church because he was concerned about my thirteen-year-old daughter, Carrie.

I was baffled by the call. Carrie was a straight "A" student, had never had a behavior problem, and was well liked by everybody.

When I met with the pastor, he told me Carrie had confided in him that she had been molested. I was totally shocked. She never acted like there was a problem when she was home, yet my pastor said that she was suicidal and needed to get help right away. How could I have missed that?

The next two and a half years were filled with psychologists and psychiatrists and an endless pursuit to find healing for my broken, battered daughter. The more Carrie hurt, the more I hurt. It was a roller coaster ride of emotions, splattered with "whys," "what ifs," and "if onlys" at every turn.

Though I had always been a Christian, I found out what real faith is all about in this painful time in our lives. It was in the midst of all of the heartache that I started to desperately reach out and seek God.

While we were under the counsel of various psychologists and psychiatrists, Carrie attempted suicide on three separate occasions over the span of two and half years. She was suffering, and I was helpless to do anything about it. And, after all this time, neither I nor anyone else, for that matter, knew who had molested her. It was a secret that she kept locked deep in herself, and it was destroying her.

Then one day the youth pastor shot and killed himself.

He was loved and respected by both the church and the community, and his suicide impacted everyone. I remember sobbing, along with everybody else, at his funeral. His wife was now widowed and his son fatherless. It was a horrible tragedy that affected all of us, especially Carrie. She instantly got worse. Her behavior manifested in eating disorders, paranoia, and social detachment. She wanted to be totally covered by layers of clothing, she could no longer cope with everyday life, and so at the age of seventeen, we admitted her to a psychiatric hospital.

After six months in the hospital, the insurance ran out. The psychiatrists told me my Carrie would never get better, never recover, and she should be institutionalized.

By now Carrie was in a catatonic state, and it seemed there was no hope left. I was distraught at their prognosis and felt agony for my daughter's life.

When I first found out that Carrie had been molested, I accused a certain man in our church. He was a touchy-feely type of guy, and although my daughter had never said he did it, we believed she had intimated as much. Carrie's hospitalization, however, allowed the truth to come out. The man who had molested her from the age of nine through thirteen had been the "beloved" youth pastor.

The pieces of the puzzle started to fit. The day before he killed himself, Carrie had confronted him. He threatened her that if she told anyone, he would commit suicide. Then, when he did take his life, Carrie blamed herself, and it reflected in her worsened condition after his death.

But God had plans for Carrie.

One night during the worst of all this, I woke up and felt God near. I sensed that I needed to start praising and thanking Him for my Carrie's life and what He would do, no matter what.

The next morning I went to a women's group at our church and shared what I was feeling. A friend had the same conviction. We agreed we should start praising and thanking God, and not stop.

There was an excitement among my friends and fellow church members. They knew that God was going to intervene in the whole situation. Their certainty encouraged me even more.

Two days later, I went to the hospital to meet with Carrie's doctors.

As I walked into the conference room I noticed their smiling faces. They told me they had surprisingly good news for me. Carrie had come out of the catatonic state, and they were going to release her to go home.

I was amazed and overjoyed that God was intervening and helping heal my daughter so quickly.

I home schooled Carrie until she was ready to go back to high school. She was still seeing psychologists and taking medication, but she had made significant strides, and it was apparent that God was answering our prayers. She re-entered high school in her senior year, and she graduated valedictorian of her class!

Although she continued to battle the ghosts of her past, she went on to university and graduated cum laude, then on to graduate school to get her master's degree and her Ph.D. in child psychology.

God is so amazing, and He did indeed have plans for Carrie. I still marvel at how far she has come.

Today Carrie is married with three children and works in children's research at a local hospital.

I learned so much through our tragedy. Juggling other family relationships during that time was often difficult and exhausting, but the family united behind me and was a real support as we sought help for our hurting Carrie.

Though I never felt deserted by God, I often felt as if I was in a "parenthesis" - like God had me on hold.

I think the biggest struggle I faced was hopelessness. I despaired over whether the situation would ever get any better. My daughter's wounds seemed beyond repair, and it all felt humanly impossible. BUT GOD . . . those are two very important words! God can do the impossible - and that's exactly what He did in Carrie's life!

It was in the impossible that God met us in a very real and special way!

"Rejoice always, pray without ceasing,
in everything give thanks; for this is
the will of God in Christ Jesus for you."
1 Thessalonians 5:16-18

THINK ABOUT THIS

How is it that within the walls of the church there can be such evil? You would think that if our children could be safe anywhere, the church would be the place where we could trust people, and yet it's not a rare occurrence in any church or denomination for a travesty such as this one to happen. Churches are just buildings, and pastors are just people. The real question is whether or not God is living in the hearts of the people and their pastor.

We hear story after story of those who have been hurt in one way or another by a church or someone in it, and God aches over every person that has suffered under the name of the Church. The Bible says that it would be better for someone to have a millstone tied around his or her neck and then thrown into the sea than to hurt one of His children (Matthew 18:6). God hates sin and the pain it causes His children. If we were assaulted at a mall, would we never go back? The truth is we would be more cautious, but we would go back.

If you think of all the bad one man could inflict on a little girl, then think of all the good one man of God could have on the life of the same little girl. God's greatest desire is for His church to be that safe harbor for His children. Don't let one man's evil inside the church close the door of your heart to all churches forevermore. God wants to use the body of believers in your life to be your encouragement and support in the midst of a fallen world. We must continue to seek God, for He is faithful – always!

QUESTIONS WE SHOULD ASK

Have you ever had an ungodly experience with a Christian or a church? Explain.

Are you living through an overwhelming situation, and the thought of praising God at this moment feels beyond comprehension?

In whom do you put your trust?

Appendix . . .

Church, Praise, Protection, Healing

five

M I C H A E L ' S   S T O R Y

A Square Peg in a Round World

*"That day I made a decision to just exist in this life,
to get through it, and to spend the rest of my time dreaming
about a place where I was happy, popular, and influential."*

Some people are just born popular. You know the type. They are a magnet, attracting others by their winsome personality, charm, or good looks. It all just flows so naturally for them. There is never a loss of friends, dates, or good times. We all know that they are going places, right? They are the future leaders of the world - the future CEOs, the future entrepreneurs, and the future famous entertainers or sports figures.

But not everyone fits into this category. I was skinny, nerdy (yes, I wore horn-rimmed glasses), and black. I didn't fit in with the black culture because I didn't have the "coolness." I was intimidated by the attitude of my fellow black brothers, and I just couldn't cut it when it came to image.

Whether it was my sister or my friends, I was constantly taunted because I was different, and yet, I did not lack the presence of people in my life. My father was a local pastor and community leader whose driving hope was to bridge the gap between the black and white communities. From an early age, my siblings and I were carted off to numerous community events and social functions. Today I credit these experiences with teaching me how to function in both cultures.

I had a lot of white friends. Besides listening to black musical groups, I also liked the Beatles, Elton John, and the Bee Gees! I was extremely insecure, and though I sometimes felt more comfortable around my white friends, I really believed I didn't fit in with them either. I was lost somewhere between a black world and a white world.

My insecurities grew as I did, and my self-esteem continued to sink. I remember one particular day in middle school when my science teacher called out the names of each student along with their grade. When she got to me she said, "Michael Delaney — F as in frog." That just cut me below the knees.

There was always something in my life that told me other people were better. Growing up in a lower middle class family, I could not do many of the things that my white friends could do. I couldn't go to camp or participate in most of the field trips that the other kids took for granted. From my perspective, money was another barrier separating me from everybody else.

All in all, life as a preacher's kid was not easy. In high school, it was always a source of ridicule. In my mind, being my father's son meant I couldn't have any fun. Who wants to hang with the preacher's kid anyway? The very things that matter the most in high school - popularity, dating, and parties - did not coexist with my background. I didn't do the things other kids did, not because I had such high personal morals, but because I didn't have the guts to rebel, and I felt the pressure to rightly represent my dad, the pastor.

Some days all I could do was feel sorry for myself. On the outside, the taunts and teasing from the guys and girls at school never let up. On the inside, I wanted to feel okay about myself, but the truth was I was only becoming more and more self-conscious.

One day I got up and looked in the mirror. I hated the mirror, but more so, I hated the person I saw looking back at me. That day I made a decision to just exist in this life, to get through it, and to spend the rest of my time dreaming about a place where I was happy, popular, and influential. Eventually my new world became just as lonely, leaving me feeling even more helpless and insecure.

I tried dating, but only had a couple of dates throughout high school. I invited a girl to a graduation party. I actually was able to buy a new suit. It was the first one I ever had in high school. While we were on the date, I put my arm around her, and she started laughing. I knew she wasn't laughing with me, but at me. I went home and never spoke about it again. Yet, inside, it shot more fear, anger, and rejection into my heart. I eventually gave up on the idea of dating altogether.

After high school, I started working for different companies and attending a Christian college. Although I got good grades, I hated college. I went because I thought I was supposed to go. I really didn't enjoy reading the Bible. I had a very negative view of Christianity. It just seemed like a bunch of rules and regulations to me.

Part of the problem was that I had a mixed-up view of God and a mixed-up view of myself. God, to me, was this heavy-handed person who was just waiting to punish me if I made the wrong move. It's a lot of pressure to keep a tyrant God happy. Little did I know that my impression of God had a lot to do with the impression I had of myself.

Then one extraordinary day, my outlook on God, life, and myself began to change. I was invited to go to Amsterdam to a Billy Graham Evangelistic Conference with a group from my church. The trip lasted 30 days. In the course of that time, I experienced something I had never felt before – unconditional love and acceptance. It was more than an incredible experience. The conference was the beginning of the end of years of debilitating insecurities, inferiorities, and fears. It genuinely was the first time I felt totally okay and wanted for just being Michael.

One particular moment at the conference is permanently etched in my mind. Billy Graham walked down the hallway and looked at my name badge. He said, "Hello, Michael," and we exchanged some kind words. Then he said he would see me after his radio interview. Of course, I thought, "He will be too busy to do that." About a half hour later, he came walking down the hall, walked up to me, put his hand on my shoulder, looked into my eyes, and said, "Michael, God bless you, God loves you, and I'm glad you're here." Even today, it brings joy to my heart when I think of that day. He had no way of knowing that his acceptance of me was a major contributor to a change in my attitude and in my life.

I came to realize that God was not a tyrant, but a loving Father who cared about me. I started going to a new church that really focused on the Bible, and, for the first time in my life, I understood that I had a very wrong impression of God.

As I read the Bible, I became convinced that God was loving and gracious, and that, in turn, changed the beliefs I had about myself. Though I had grown up in the church, I never really KNEW of God's deep and personal love for me. I knew and loved Jesus, it was the Father God that I had a hard time with. Now, I not only had a better relationship with Christ, but I also saw that I was a loved and worthwhile man in Him. The pressure to fit in started to erode because I saw that I was exactly the way God meant me to be, and that was a good thing!

When the walls of self-hatred came down, I was capable of having friendships with men and women. It is really amazing what the Lord has done in my life. I started to reach out to others, and the Lord blessed me with lots of good friends. I was always a friend to anybody and everybody who would accept me. But now I was having more balanced relationships with everyone.

When I look in a mirror these days, I see someone very different. My self-hatred and insecurities have been replaced with the valuable knowledge that I am a creation of God - unique, worthwhile, and born with a purpose. And, most importantly, when I look in the mirror, I see a man who is loved by God.

The bridge that my father spent his life building (a bridge between the races) is one that unites all of us in our common human value and worth to God. We don't have to fit into a mold or a culture; all we have to do is understand who God is, and everything else falls into place. Black or white, we are loved by God, and our lives have meaning. When you come to understand that, you begin to love God, yourself, and others.

Though at times I still feel moments of insecurity, I am no longer ruled by the deep wounds of my past. In 1996, I met my future wife. Having never had a serious relationship, or much of a dating life, I saw something very different in this particular woman. We became instant friends at church. There was just something about her, and we clicked. We complemented each other and were comfortable together. I had never experienced that before.

I got married at the age of 37. More than 400 people attended my wedding from various backgrounds. To this day, my pastor tells me it is the only wedding he has ever officiated where the audience gave the couple a standing ovation. God had mended a broken man, and everyone at the wedding celebrated that fact.

Today I'm an associate pastor on staff at my church. I'm helping other wounded people to discover the love and hope that is found in Jesus. And, together with my wife, we're forging new frontiers and carrying on the work of my father and his Lord - building bridges of love throughout our community.

"I will praise You, for I am fearfully and wonderfully made;
Marvelous are Your works, And that my soul knows very well.
My frame was not hidden from You, When I was made in secret,
And skillfully wrought in the lowest parts of the earth.
Your eyes saw my substance, being yet unformed. And in Your book they
all were written, The days fashioned for me, When as yet there were none
of them. How precious also are Your thoughts to me, O God! How great
is the sum of them! If I should count them, they would be more in number
than the sand; When I awake, I am still with You."
Psalm 139:14-18

THINK ABOUT THIS

We all struggle with insecurities. Some of us are just better at disguising them than others. Sometimes we take on pride to cover our shortcomings, and other times we just hide them from the world around us.

God created each of us for a unique purpose. When we are not happy with ourselves, we need to go to God, wrestle with Him, and ask, "Why did You create me ... for what?"

Jacob, a character in the Bible, did just that. He wrestled with God until God gave him that blessing of a purpose for his future. God will do the same for you. Sometimes He just wants us to be persistent in our prayers and "wrestle" with Him a little to show that we really want what He has in store for us. Whatever it is, it will be worth the effort.

QUESTIONS WE SHOULD ASK

Is inferiority a dominating factor in your life?

Have you lived with discouragement for too long and want to find a solution?

How has your perception of God been affected by your upbringing?

Appendix ...

Inferiority, Discouragement, Jesus

six

L O U I S E ' S   S T O R Y

Living Through Grief

*"My son's death became my obsession.
I wanted to know where he was and if he was okay,
and I wanted to stay connected to him. I just couldn't let go."*

I had a wonderful, happy childhood.

I was brought up in a large, loving family by parents who actually loved each other. We lived in a nice home in a quiet Massachusetts neighborhood and went to church every Sunday. Everything in my life was picture perfect.

At the age of twelve, I met my future husband. He was very handsome and worked for my father after school. Even as children, we adored each other, and I knew that one day he would be my husband. In fact, neither of us ever dated anyone else.

When I turned eighteen, we got married. We loved married life. Eventually we added three children to our family, and we truly enjoyed our family time together. My husband became very successful in his business, and we all reaped the benefits of an affluent lifestyle. Once again everything in my life was picture perfect... well, nearly perfect.

One problem was my husband's occasional excessive drinking. He didn't think it was a problem, but I did. Then a recession hit, and finances became tight. My husband tried to hold on to the business, but ended up going bankrupt. His drinking increased, and my little world began to crumble.

I was a religious person in the sense that I went to my Catholic church every Sunday, but it was not really relevant to my life. For the most part, life had always been good to me, but when my husband lost his business and began to drink more and more, I started to pray for a miracle.

God answered my prayers.

Even though my husband never even wanted to cut back on his drinking, one day God just took the desire to drink away from him, and he never had a beer again! It made a big difference in our lives. I was excited about the restoration of our life together and felt the promise of hope that even our finances would turn around.

In reality, God was preparing us for the storm that was about to crash in us.

One summer evening, when my husband was away on a trip, I was waiting for our son Chris to arrive home from visiting a friend. It was a long drive, but he told me he should be home in time for dinner. Six o'clock rolled around, and then seven ... then eight, and still no sign of Chris. I started to worry. I called his friend, who confirmed that he had left on time. I tried to be calm and read a book, but the clock kept ticking, and my son never showed up.

At 1:00 a.m., I called the police.

While I was on the phone with the local police department, a Teletype message came in from the State Police, and I was put on hold. When the officer came back on the phone, his voice was grim, and he informed me that they were sending an officer over to the house.

I knew in my heart something was terribly wrong. The officer that came was Chris' friend, and he confirmed my heart's worst fear - that my son had died in an automobile accident.

My picture perfect world shattered in a million pieces.

My husband flew home, and family and friends flooded to the house to help make funeral arrangements and lend support. I withdrew to my bed, holding my grief inside.

I couldn't do anything after Chris died. I detached myself from everybody. My mother cared for my younger daughter and cooked the meals while I stayed in my bedroom reading and searching for answers.

The material I read had a central focus - the afterlife. I would go to the bookstore and buy every book I could on the subject. My son's death became my obsession. I wanted to know where he was and if he was okay, and I wanted to stay connected to him. I just couldn't let go.

I got involved in New Age religion and would leave the house only to go to seminars about how to contact the dead.

Though I had gone to a Catholic church my whole life, I had no understanding of God or life beyond the grave. I was desperate to know what happens after death, but instead of turning to God, I turned to the occult. I didn't know what I was getting myself into at the time because I was so focused on wanting to know about my son.

About a month after Chris died, my husband and I lost our home and our cars to another bankruptcy. We were forced to move several times within a few short months, but, despite the upheaval, I stayed numb to the process. My only concern was my son and how to contact him.

Soon books were not enough for me. Then a friend introduced me to the Ouija board. The very first time I tried it (with my friend), I believed that I had contacted my son. I had put my fingers lightly on the viewer. As it moved, it spelled out, "Hi Ma." The more questions I asked, the more answers I got. In fact, I would even test the Ouija board by asking questions that I believed only Chris would know, and I would get answers like, "Stop testing me Ma." I was convinced that I was communicating with my child.

I consulted the Ouija board a couple of times a day for almost a year. At first it seemed right and good. The board gave me a sense of hope that my son was all right and that I was still connected to him. I started getting out of bed and mingling with people again. But my rebound didn't last.

I had no idea that the Ouija board was an open door into the demonic spirit world. Unfortunately, I was immersed in it. What I was unaware of at the time was that I was never communicating with my son, but with evil spiritual forces that were very real and dangerous.

Everything was falling apart around my family and me. My husband could not make a living in New England, so he moved us to Florida where he took a job as a developer. Two months later, he was laid off. Within the course of a year, we moved eleven times.

I began to rapidly deteriorate mentally and physically.

I couldn't find anybody in Florida who had the power to do the Ouija board with me, so for a while I stopped. I got very depressed and distraught. The occult practices were taking a toll on me. Even though I had stopped consulting the board, the damage had been done. I was suicidal by now, and day by day my thoughts became increasingly more dark and hopeless.

I went to a psychiatrist who put me on Prozac, but it did nothing. I could not stand being alive, and my mind continually turned to death. The woman that had once thought life was wonderful was now sinking in a world of despair and desiring death. I always had the urge to drive my car into a pole or a tree. I never talked to anyone about the torment I was going through in my mind, and I didn't know what to do about it. Doctors did not help, tranquilizers failed, and even loving family members were unable to help me find hope, but God knew I was in trouble, and He was working behind the scenes for me.

We ended up moving to a new neighborhood into a house that we really could not afford. The woman who owned the home wanted so much for us to take it that she reduced the rent and even painted it inside and out. The whole situation was like a miracle.

One afternoon I was driving home from the car repair shop when suddenly the air conditioning quit and the windows would not roll down - the exact same problems I had just paid the mechanic to fix. I stopped the car and burst into tears. I knew I was at my breaking point and that I could not go on one more day.

The very next day my new neighbor was walking her dog, when the dog came to a stop in front of my house, so she walked to my front door and rang the doorbell.

I opened the door, and in no time I was crying on her shoulder. She sensed that I was on the brink of a nervous breakdown so she invited me to her Bible study the next morning.

The speaker happened to be talking about demonic activity. I listened intently and began to wonder about all of the activities I had dabbled in over the last year, especially the Ouija board. When the study was over, I went up to talk with her. I asked her if she thought the Ouija board was satanic. She had a horrified look on her face, walked me home, and came into my house. We sat down, and she prayed. It was that evening that I asked God to truly help me, and He did.

My neighbor started taking me to her church on a regular basis, and the woman that led the Bible study befriended me as well. I bought my first Bible and read it daily. The Bible introduced me to God, and it was new life to my soul. I could tell that God was beginning to work in my life, but there was still one hindrance that had to be taken care of - all the paraphernalia of my journey into the occult.

My friend came over and rid my house of every trace of the Ouija board, the books, and the notebooks that detailed every message that supposedly came from my son. Then she prayed that God would bless our home.

That night was the first time since Chris died that I slept through the night. Finally I had peace, and I could relax. I finally knew the truth about my son's death from God's Word.

I found healing from my sorrow when I met God. Now I am helping those who have suffered the loss of a loved one, letting them know that they can turn to God and find comfort, peace, and compassion for their grieving hearts.

"And the person who turns to mediums and familiar
spirits, to prostitute himself with them, I will set My
face against that person and cut him off from his people.
Consecrate yourselves therefore, and be holy,
for I am the Lord your God."
Leviticus 20:6,7

THINK ABOUT THIS

Death is so final. We want it to make sense, but it doesn't, especially when it hits our children. We search for answers from our friends, but they don't have them. We go to family, but they just cry with us. Then we go to God.

God knows our end on earth is our beginning in heaven, yet He mourns with us because He knows what it's like to lose a child for a season. After all, He sent His Son to earth for 33 years.

The Bible instructs us to "Trust in the Lord with all your heart and lean not on your own understanding" (Proverbs 3:5). We will never understand why God takes our young ones from us in the middle of life, but if we will just trust Him, He will heal us, and help us to go on living.

QUESTIONS WE SHOULD ASK

Have you faced the death of a loved one and are looking for answers? What answers has God given you?

Have you been dabbling in the occult and wondering what you've gotten mixed up in?

Has grief become your constant companion and you're ready to say good-bye to it?

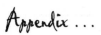 Appendix . . .

Death, Occult, Grief

seven

D A L E ' S   S T O R Y

The Secret of Success

*"Even though I had accepted Christ, we struggled
in our marriage from the beginning. We fought terribly.
There had been a vital change in my life,
but I still struggled when it came to relationships."*

My childhood was normal.

I did not come from a divorced home or an abusive background. I did what every other kid did - I went to school and I played. My father was not very religious, although my mother was a deeply spiritual person. I had one older brother who spent his time harassing me, like older brothers often do. All in all, everything was typical. It was after I graduated from high school that my life got complicated.

When I was eighteen, my dad died unexpectedly from a heart attack. He was 51. His death shocked our family, and although I grieved, I spent much of my time trying to cover up my true feelings.

It was a front that I would become more comfortable with over time.

I joined the Air Force at the suggestion of my older brother, Rodney, and was stationed in North Africa for four years. The military taught me discipline - something I incorporated in my business life but not in my personal life. After leaving the Air Force, I moved to Florida where I worked and went to college.

Success excited me. I started working with my brother on different projects. My brother was intelligent, a great salesman, and a motivator of people. I was envious of his talents, but at the same time enjoyed being on a tag team with him as we chased after the brass ring.

By the age of 30, I had yet to settle down. I had two priorities in life - money and women. I had a reputation as a womanizer, and I had numerous one-night stands, but no serious relationship, nor did I want one.

Then I met Ann.

She was divorced with four young kids between the ages of three and eight. Ann was pretty and also the first woman I had ever respected. Life had been difficult for her, and I really wanted to take care of her and her kids.

We got married, but our marriage was in trouble from the start. I was immature and selfish. I was too self-centered to be a good husband or father. My hunger and thirst for money and success drove me to work seven days a week.

After just two years, we called it quits. It was a bad time for me because I felt miserable about the marriage ending and guilty over the pain I had caused Ann and the children. For the first time in many years, I allowed myself to feel my emotions and cry, but I quickly put my mask back on and continued to hide my inner feelings while I strived to keep up with my success-driven lifestyle.

I maintained a relationship with the kids and a friendship with Ann. Around that same time I started getting involved with the "social" drug scene, even though I hid the effects pretty well.

I also began attending local churches looking for something more for my life. There I met Adrian, a flight attendant and a Christian. When I met her, I thought I had found what I was looking for. We dated off and on for a couple of years.

Adrian struggled with our relationship. Although we had all the material possessions money could buy, she wanted marriage and my love and respect, which I found difficult to give. I looked fine on the outside – a successful businessman - but inside I was hurting. I was still full of my own selfishness, which made it hard to care about anyone else. Ironically, I felt empty.

Then, one day, something got my attention.

While enjoying a day out on the water in my friend's boat, I was thrown out of the boat and into a sea wall. As doctors worked feverishly on me in the emergency room, Adrian waited nervously with friends and family. It was determined that my neck was fractured and I would have to undergo a serious operation.

Adrian, who had been a Christian for many years by this time, feared for my salvation. We both realized how close I had come to death and knew I needed to get right with God.

Adrian had shared the gospel with me many times, but I had never accepted Christ personally. She knew she could not marry me until I became a believer because there were just too many things we couldn't agree on, so she prayed fervently for me to accept Christ.

Before my operation I asked her to have someone from her church come and speak with me about God. I was ready to ask Him to be a part of my life. He had gotten my attention.

I went through the surgery and spent more than a month in the hospital. After I was released, Adrian and I tied the knot.

Even though I had accepted Christ, we struggled in our marriage from the beginning. We fought constantly. There had been a vital change in my life, but I still struggled when it came to relationships. I was involved with Youth for Christ and went to a conference that dealt with commitment in marriage. I had no doubt God was speaking to me there.

I started going to counseling, and both Adrian and I began going to church regularly. It wasn't long before we saw an improvement in our marriage. God was changing our wants and our desires. I stopped using drugs, and we both stopped our excessive social drinking. Then we began to pray together. We could tell that God was working to make a real difference in our lives.

I wish my story ended there, but it doesn't. We had more difficulties and harder trials to go through in the years to come.

It wasn't long before Adrian found out that she had lymphoma and less than a year to live.

When you get news like that, it really jolts everything into perspective fast. Those things that we hold so dear - material possessions, pride, and career - become so insignificant, and you quickly discover just how genuine your faith in God is. I battled my doubts, asked why, and was angry about Adrian's cancer. It was a very painful time, filled with bouts of depression, but we did not give up on our faith. We both turned to God, and He met us in the midst of our pain and panic.

God used Adrian's cancer to heal our marriage and create a deeper bond between us. We cried and we prayed together, and as I, this former, very self-centered man, cared for Adrian during her illness, she soon realized my deep love for her.

Adrian also encountered God in a way that she had never known Him before. Many times she would be up all night in agony and yet enjoying the most beautiful times of prayer and quiet with the Lord. She would say that all her pain would melt in the light of His glory and grace. Looking back, she says that she would not change one moment of what she endured. "He healed me in more ways than one," she says.

Life is still not perfect, and it is not always easy, but God wants to fill our lives with His love, His peace, and His joy. He is in control and wants to heal our sorrows, our relationships, and our wounds.

Adrian and I have been married for twenty years. From the beginning, she prayed for God to give her a supernatural joy and acceptance of His will for our lives, and God did just that. We live in Florida and are active in our church. We are a living testament that success is not material acquisition but spiritual gain, and that God can work through even the most unbearable circumstances in our lives to bring about His glory and peace.

"Likewise the Spirit also helps in our weaknesses.
For we do not know what we should pray for as we ought,
but the Spirit Himself makes intercession for us with
groanings which cannot be uttered."
Romans 8:26

THINK ABOUT THIS

We all tend to think that the world revolves around us. If you could see the world through your neighbor's eyes, it would look very different from the way you perceive it. Even as children, we expect the things of this world to fulfill our own needs. It's part of being human. The problem with selfishness is that it destroys relationships and hurts those around us. It's something we quite often do not see in ourselves, and yet others can see it in us very clearly. It is also the one thing God requires us to give up in order to receive Him.

The Bible says Jesus is "the Son of God, who loved me and gave Himself for me"(Galatians 2:20). Jesus did it first. He knew it would be hard for us, so He led the way, so to speak. The Bible also says, "Come to me, all you who are weary and burdened, and I will give you rest"(Matthew 11:28). It takes a lot of effort to satisfy our own selfishness. Try giving the burden of your selfish desires over to God, and He will give you a rest and satisfaction that last.

QUESTIONS WE SHOULD ASK

Are you considered a self-centered or others-centered person? Why?

What has brought you permanent happiness?

When facing a physical and/or emotional illness, how do you handle it?

Appendix . . .

Self-Centeredness, Materialism, Depression, Healing

eight

C H R I S T I N E ' S   S T O R Y

There Is Freedom!

"I never felt safe as a girl because
every man I met treated me as the object of his desire.
Women seemed to be the only safe option in relationships."

My heart pounded as the Sunday school teacher asked us to break into small groups and discuss how we might reach the homosexual community for Christ. I had often wondered if everyone knew my secret. Now I would find out for sure. In my group of four, Rachel spoke first, "I don't have any compassion for homosexuals."

My heart sank.

Mark chimed in, "I don't have any compassion for homosexuals either, and I think AIDS is God's judgment against homosexuals."

These two seemed so smug, so arrogant. Anger burned within me, and I vowed not to speak. My friend, Robert, who knew I was a former homosexual, spoke next, "Christine, what do you think?"

I shot him a look that could kill, then I took a deep breath, and shared my secret. You could have heard the proverbial pin drop as the looks on their faces told me they were embarrassed and truly sorry. What they didn't understand was that I, like most homosexuals, never wanted to be gay. It just sort of happened.

I grew up in a home where women were either the object of a man's lust or the victim of his abuse. My father was addicted to pornography, and he was physically and verbally abusive to my mother. I still remember the night I saw him hit her with a tennis racket. It was late, and they were fighting again. I couldn't sleep with all the yelling. I got out of bed, tiptoed past all my stuffed animals, out the bedroom door and down the hallway, where I peered into the living room. My father was glaring at my mother with a cold, angry look. Then he raised the tennis racket that was in his hand and swung it at her, hitting the left side of her body. She stood there motionless and did not fight back. In that moment I vowed in my heart that I would never let a man hurt me like that. I would be tougher and stronger than them.

I hated being a girl because I didn't want to be a victim like my mom. I mistakenly believed that to be feminine was to be weak, so I gravitated toward the masculine. My older brother was my childhood hero. I wanted to be just like him. I hung out with him whenever he would let me, wore his hand-me-down clothes, and even copied his handwriting style. I wanted to be anything but a girl.

As a natural athlete, I excelled in every sport I attempted, from tennis to little league baseball to sandlot football. I was accepted as one of the guys and often mistaken for a boy. I refused to go by my full name, Christine, because it was obviously a girl's name. Instead I went by "Chris."

My parents divorced when I was twelve and sent me to live with relatives, where an older cousin molested me. This did not help my already warped view of men.

Growing up, there were other incidences where men took advantage of me. I never felt safe as a girl because every man I met treated me as the object of his desire. Women seemed to be the only safe option in relationships.

My first gay relationship began in high school. It was exhilarating and met a need in my life because for the first time I really felt loved. I was a lesbian for six years and believed I would always be gay. I didn't know that change was possible, but, while in college, I met some Christians who showed me an even better love - the love that God had for me.

Though I was in a homosexual relationship, I played on a friend's church softball team. One teammate, Kelly, knew I was gay because my masculine appearance and mannerisms gave me away, but she never preached to me. She just loved me and prayed for me.

In time I was drawn by the love my fellow teammates had for each other and for me. It seemed so pure and so right. I became interested in spiritual things and asked Kelly to help me study the Bible. She readily agreed, and we met weekly to study the book of John.

One Sunday night in October 1989, Kelly led me in a prayer of salvation as I knelt beside my bed in my dorm at the University of Tampa. I didn't feel any different when I stood up, but deep down I knew something had changed. I knew I meant business with God. I wanted Him more than my homosexuality.

Becoming a Christian didn't instantly resolve my homosexual orientation. It was only the beginning of my journey. I broke up with my girlfriend, yet continued to struggle with unwanted same-sex attractions.

Thankfully, I found out about Exodus International, a ministry that helps people overcome their homosexuality, and began to attend a local support group in Tampa. That's where I discovered the root causes of my homosexual desires - things like sexual abuse, gender confusion, breakdown in the relationship with the same-sex parent, an abusive father, and peer rejection.

The real healing came as I met godly, strong women in the church who dismantled my belief that to be feminine was to be weak. I also met men who treated me with dignity and respect. This freed me to embrace my gender and stop rejecting God's design. I even started going by my full name, Christine, because I no longer wanted to hide the fact that I was a girl.

Change happened from the inside out. First, the wrong beliefs about men and women were put to rest. I learned that being female is not a liability. Then I began to outwardly identify with women, experimenting with things like make-up, clothes, and purses.

Others noticed my progress and encouraged me. I'll never forget the time Robert approached me in church and said, smiling, "Christine, this is the first time you don't look like a boy in a dress." Though it didn't come out right, I knew he meant well, and it let me know I was making progress.

The key to my healing was developing healthy same-sex friendships. As I did this, my sexual attractions for women naturally diminished because I found what I was looking for all along - love, intimacy, and connection.

With God's help and the support of caring people, I have been walking in freedom from homosexuality for over 10 years now. I know that change is possible because I am a changed life.

"Brethren, I do not count myself to have apprehended;
but one thing I do, forgetting those things which are
behind and reaching forward to those things which
are ahead, I press toward the goal for the prize
of the upward call of God in Christ Jesus."
Philippians 3:13-14

THINK ABOUT THIS

Are we reaching out to the homosexual community, or have we isolated them and made them feel unwelcome in our churches? Christine was fortunate enough to have Christians in her life that reached out to her, and it radically changed her life. God met her right where she was.

If you are a homosexual, then we apologize for the attitudes that many individuals have toward you as a person. You were fearfully and wonderfully made by a God that truly loves you. We all have sin in our lives, and, in God's eyes, sin is sin. We all need to turn from sin and live as God would have us. If we spent a little more time working on our own sin instead of judging others, then we could be used by God to encourage others.

The religious men of Jesus' day asked Him, "Why do You eat and drink with ...sinners?" Jesus answered and said to them, "Those who are well have no need of a physician, but those who are sick. I have not come to call the righteous, but sinners, to repentance" (Luke 5:30-32). God wants to teach you how to have a relationship with Him that will be far more rewarding than any sin in your life. Give God a chance to change your life like He changed Christine's.

QUESTIONS WE SHOULD ASK

At what times in your life have you felt the most isolated and lonely?

Has sexual immorality been something that you have struggled with? How have you dealt with it?

Is homosexuality a deep dark secret for you and something you would like to find help for?

Appendix ...

Loneliness, Sexual Immorality, Homosexuality

nine

JAKE'S STORY

The Battle of a Teen

*"Again, I considered taking my own life.
I was so empty inside. I decided to get my friend's gun
and end my sorry life."*

Childhood is supposed to be a time of carefree activity and unabated innocence, but when that innocence is stripped away, so is the carefree life. In an instant, life becomes pitiful and burdensome, and a child loses his childhood for good. That's what happened to me, and this is my story.

My dad was in the Navy and proud of it. When I was a young kid, my family moved back to upstate New York to be near my father's family. Early on, I felt the ugliness of prejudice and racism. My father is black, and my mother is white - a racial partnership that was not at all accepted in the early sixties.

Yet in my neighborhood, I thrived. I had a friendship with my Grandpa Joe, who paid more attention to me than my own father, and I had a friendship with him that kept me going.

My family went to church because that was what we were supposed to do. My dad wasn't a bad man, but we just didn't have much of a relationship. In fact, from the age of eleven on, we had no relationship at all. This bothered me. Like any other kid, I figured out a way to adjust to the way things were - that is, until the day my cousin molested me, betrayed my trust, and stole my childhood. It's amazing, looking back, how my whole life changed in a flash. He destroyed my identity, took away my sense of self worth, and introduced me to the perverted world of pornography.

After that, my life began to spiral down with a steady acceleration.

By the age of twelve, I already had a reputation of being a "partyer." I began experimenting with sex and would do anything to get a girl's attention. In fact, at one of my first parties, I allowed a girl to pierce my ear just to get her to notice me.

In middle school, I started coming home drunk. I thought I was so cool, and soon I took up smoking pot as well. In my mind, the more I partied, the more I was accepted and liked. I didn't get it that trying to find acceptance would actually end up isolating me and driving me to despair.

By high school, I was addicted to drugs, sex, girls, and pornography. As with any addiction, I needed a stronger and stronger fix to get the same thrills and highs. I graduated from pot to cocaine and then on to crack. Meanwhile my sexual appetite was becoming more and more weird.

By eighteen, I was a full-blown addict. I was also something else - I was ashamed and confused. Though I knew my behavior was wrong, I really didn't know what normal was either. My whole outlook on relationships was messed up and my sexual desires and relations were perverted.

My parents got fed up with my behavior, and my dad wouldn't have anything to do with me. I thought he was a jerk and wanted my mother to divorce him.

Then something happened to my mom and dad. They found God, and it began to reflect in their attitudes. Instead of fighting, they started to back each other up. There was a spirit of unity in our home that had never been there before. Along with their new partnership came a renewed interest in disciplining their children - something that did not go over well with me.

My life was headed nowhere. I was busy selling drugs on my school campus and had no desire to study or think about getting a job. It was Grandpa Joe that sat me down one day and tried to bring a dose of reality into my life.

He told me I needed to do something with my life and that maybe I should go to automotive tech school since my grades weren't good enough to get me into college, so that's what I did.

In tech school, I met a girl. She got my interest to the point of considering marriage. After a semester of school, I announced to my parents that I was going to marry her. I packed up all of my belongings, quit school, and took my new girlfriend back home with me.

When we got there, my parents refused to let me in the house, so I turned to my drug dealer and rented an apartment from him. Besides trimming trees and doing odd jobs, I spent my time doing drugs and drinking. My girlfriend was talking about God a lot, and after a while she got tired of my drinking and drugging and went home to be with her family and go back to church. I decided I probably needed to try and clean up my act, so I moved back in with my parents and started going to church also.

The only thing was, I was still getting high and acting like a hypocrite.

After two months, my girlfriend called me to say she was moving back to town to be near me. She lived with a youth pastor and his family. The closer she got to God, the more she tried reaching out to me, but by now drugs were my god, and I just couldn't give up my addiction.

Then my girlfriend started seeing another guy. I was a wreck when she dumped me, even though I knew she had continually tried to reach out to me, and I was the fool who didn't want to give up my lifestyle for her.

The impact of losing her was overwhelming. The youth pastor suggested that I move out of state, but I couldn't. I spent four months getting wasted on cocaine instead, and my personality kept unraveling. Thoughts of suicide invaded my mind. After one very desperate night, I got in my car and drove from New York to Florida.

Changing cities did nothing to change my circumstances or my addictions. I thought that by leaving I could escape my problems, but I found other drug dealers, another set of friends to party with, and more girls to have sex with. It was the same lifestyle in a different location.

At one point I was dating a fifteen-year-old girl and a 38-year-old married woman at the same time. One night, I got a phone call from the woman's husband, a police officer, who threatened to kill me.

Again, I considered taking my own life. I was so empty inside. I decided to get my friend's gun and end my sorry life.

I dropped to the floor and started to sob.

After crying it out for a while, the Bible stories from my childhood church days started coming back to my mind. I asked God, if He was real, to change my life. There was a feeling of warmth and love and light and peace that just seemed to flood the room.

I looked at my drug scale and noticed that it was clean, and right next to it was my dust-covered Bible given to me when I was twelve years old. I had never even looked at it. I went over and picked it up. On the inside of the cover was a piece of paper that said, "God is greater than any problem I might have." I slept that night like a baby.

I had met God.

Following that eventful night, I started talking with a Christian I had met at the garage where I worked. He invited me to his church. Before too long, I got excited about going to church and reading my Bible.

My life started to improve. The craving for drugs left me. For the first time in my life, I stopped using. I moved out of my dealer's apartment and in with another Christian guy in a better neighborhood.

Three months later, I went back to New York and reconciled with my family. I asked my father and grandfather for forgiveness. In fact, it was the first time that I ever told my parents I loved them.

I also went to my cousin who had molested me and talked with him. I told him that I had forgiven him for what he had done. It was one more step in putting my past behind me.

Then I went back to Florida and stayed. I got involved with my church and started a new life. Today I am married with two children and have served as a youth pastor for almost seven years. My life is a testimony of God's grace and love and an example of the power of transformation that's possible when a messed-up, fallen-down guy meets Almighty God.

"But God has chosen the foolish things of the world
to put to shame the wise, and God has chosen the
weak things of the world to put to shame the
things which are mighty."
1 Corinthians 1:27

THINK ABOUT THIS

Jake's story is not unique. Drugs, sex, and rock 'n roll are everywhere. Kids, younger and younger, are experimenting with them, and parents are not around enough to even notice. What is the answer?

The Bible says, "...what I want to do I do not do, but what I hate I do"(Romans 7:15). It's that simple - without God we are victims of our own earthly desires - desires that temporarily bring happiness, but eventually lead to our destruction.

We can get so busy in our lives, working at our jobs, managing our homes, and enjoying our social lives that we forget to realize we are often being watched by the eyes of the next generation. That's one reason Jake has devoted his new life to working with teens. He wants to help other kids like himself in the teen battle. We all have people we influence. Look for an opportunity to reach out to young people. You could spend time with them, talk with them, or laugh with them. You just might make all the difference in their lives.

QUESTIONS WE SHOULD ASK

What has influenced your self-image over the years?

Have you dealt with childhood abuse of one kind or another? Where are you in the healing process?

Has an addiction invaded your life and made you captive to it? What are some of the steps you can take to break free?

Appendix ...

Poor Self Image, Child Abuse, Addiction

ten

C A R O L ' S   S T O R Y

I Did it All for Love

"Angry and hurt, I threw a drink in Dave's face. Then I looked my husband right in the eyes and said, 'Don't you ever bother coming home again,' and stormed out of the party."

I was always the romantic type.

When I met Dave at the age of thirteen, I knew I was in love. I saw him across the room at the football kickoff dance, and when he came up to me and asked me to go for a ride in his car, it was the beginning of a long, tumultuous, and often heartbreaking relationship.

At the age of sixteen, I got pregnant.

Our parents met together and three options - abortion, marriage, or adoption - were discussed. Abortion was difficult, as it was illegal and I was already five months pregnant. Marriage was frowned upon since we were both so young. Our parents decided it was best to send me to a home for unwed mothers where I could have the baby and then give it up for adoption.

I was a senior in high school, a cheerleader, and popular. The thought of going to an unwed mothers' home frightened and saddened me, but I had no other choice.

When it came time for me to deliver my baby, I had to have a Cesarean section. Along with the surgery came blood tests. Because I was RH negative and Dave was RH positive, the doctors warned us that if we ever got married, we would be discouraged from having any other children.

Here I was, only sixteen years old, undergoing my first surgery, having a baby, unwed, and being told that if I were to marry the man I loved, I would not be able to have any other children. I felt ruined, but I would have much more to endure.

In a state of emotional trauma, and having second thoughts about giving the baby up for adoption, my parents and I agreed to keep the baby and made arrangements to take care of it at a friend's home.

I delivered a beautiful, eight-pound baby girl and came through the surgery with flying colors. Eight days later, Dave's father came to the home and gave me an ultimatum. He told me that if I chose to go through with my decision to keep the baby, Dave was going to go into the priesthood, and I would never see him again. I loved Dave, and now I was being forced to choose between him and my new baby daughter. Fearfully, I signed the papers and gave my baby up for adoption. But then, as I held her in my arms for the last time, I vowed never to see Dave again.

My parents were upset at my decision. It didn't matter. I was angry at Dave and didn't want him near me. My body was scarred, and my heart was broken.

He kept calling and pursuing me, and finally I agreed to date him again. We never spoke about our baby or the adoption.

About sixteen months later, I got pregnant again. This time there was no option. Dave and I married and kept the pregnancy a secret.

The large wedding embarrassed me. I felt like I was living a lie. In fact, I even thought about suicide. Even though I loved Dave, there was a lot of hurt packed into our relationship.

When we first got married, Dave worked as a purchasing agent. Within two years we had two daughters. Considering all that we had been through, our marriage was working out pretty well. Seven years later, he landed a job as a salesman and began traveling. It wasn't long before he got caught up in drinking, pornography, rakish activities, and extramarital affairs.

I had no idea that he was leading this kind of life until some years later when he came home one day and told me that he had a venereal disease and that I needed to go and get tested.

Dave's parents were living in Florida, and they wanted us to move there to be near them. Thinking that his parents would be a good influence on him, I agreed to make the move. So, after ten years of marriage, Dave, the children, and I packed our bags and moved south. I didn't understand at the time that without an inner heart change, Dave's acting out would not miraculously end just because he was in a different environment.

Dave's office in Florida was located next door to "Big Daddy's Lounge," which he began to frequent often. His escapades did not end with a few drinks after work. Soon he fell in love with his secretary and flaunted their relationship, even in front of me. One New Year's Eve, we were invited to a party, and I consented to go only if his secretary would not be there. We went, and before long she showed up.

That was the straw that broke the camel's back. Angry and desperate, I threw a drink in Dave's face. Then I looked my husband right in the eyes and said, "Don't you ever bother coming home again," and stormed out of the party.

I was through with the marriage and all its heartache. I went home and fell on the bed in my room. I felt suicidal again and called out to God, begging Him to take my life. Just then, the room seemed to light up, and I felt God speak three words to my heart, "Stay. Trust Me."

A peace came over me that I had never felt before. I slept like a lamb that night, and when I woke up the next morning I felt like a different person. I went to Dave's parents' home and told them what had happened. I knew that the Lord had spoken to me. Even though I could not trust my husband, I knew I was supposed to trust God.

I stayed in the marriage. In fact, the Lord impressed upon me to write a letter of apology to the couple who had hosted the party as well as the escort of the secretary that I had embarrassed.

Although Dave did tell me he was sorry, he had told me this before but had never changed his behavior. I told him about my experience with God and that I was going to be obedient to God, but I also told him that he had a choice to make - either he would go off with his secretary or he would stay home and be a husband and a father.

Unfortunately, Dave's heart had not changed, only mine.

I got plugged into a women's Bible study. I learned more and more about the Lord and grew to love Him more. Every day I prayed for Dave.

One day, the phone rang; it was the secretary's husband. He informed me that he had seen my husband and his wife at a local Holiday Inn and had decked Dave in the eye. Later, Dave called to tell me that he opened the medicine cabinet into his eye and didn't want me to be alarmed at his black eye.

That night I told Dave that I knew the truth behind his black eye. I also told him to get some help.

We decided to go for counseling, and two years later, while Dave was helping some of our friends move to Washington, D.C., he went to a church there and opened his heart to God. It took yet another five years before he was a changed man.

The moment of true change came when Dave read a specific Bible passage: "No temptation has overtaken you except such as is common to man; but God is faithful, who will not allow you to be tempted beyond what you are able, but with the temptation will also make the way of escape, that you may be able to bear it" (1 Corinthians 10:13). He began to realize that he wasn't the first man to struggle in this area of his life, that God had provided a way for him to overcome this, and that if he allowed God to fix him, he would become all that God created him to be. I began to see God do just that.

When Dave finally got to the end of himself, God transformed him into a man who was humble and willing to learn. God blessed me for my willingness to stay in the marriage by giving me the man I had always wanted from the very beginning.

We have been married now for 39 years. Dave is an associate pastor at our church, and together we counsel other couples that are being struck down by hardship and heartache in their marriages.

"Whoever keeps the fig tree will eat its fruit;
So he who waits on his master will be honored."
Proverbs 27:18

THINK ABOUT THIS

Relationships can be so confusing. Our emotions seem to take over our sense of logic, and we find it so difficult to find solutions to our problems. God has a plan for each and every relationship in our life. We need to seek out that plan. No two plans will be the same, just as no two relationships are the same, but God will help us find solutions if we will just ask.

Just as we have experienced heartache or sorrow in the midst of a relationship, so, too, has God experienced heartache in His relationship with humankind. We read a story like Carol's and feel the dread of being betrayed, and yet in our relationships with God, we are the adulterers. Wow, imagine that! It's so easy to take God's love for granted, and even forsake it.

God's greatest desire is to have a relationship with you. Take time today and think about your relationship with God. How have you treated Him lately; how has He treated you?

QUESTIONS WE SHOULD ASK

Have you experienced the pain of an unfaithful spouse?

What are the strengths and weaknesses of your relationship? Is God a part of it?

Do you realize the depth of God's love for you regardless of the way you live your life? Are you living a lie and don't know how to change?

Appendix...

Affair Victims, Seeking God's Will, Love of God

eleven

R O B E R T ' S   S T O R Y

Weeds of Bitterness

"Three weeks after graduating from college, I moved to Florida
with my best friend, where I began my pursuit
to be a millionaire."

I had one goal - to be wealthy.

Born and raised in West Virginia, my family life was different from most of my friends' lives. My mother became pregnant with me in the later years of her life. She already had two children, a daughter, twenty-three, and a mentally retarded daughter who was twenty-one, so the news of my arrival came as quite a shock to her.

Though loved by my parents, at the age of five I went to live with my oldest sister and her husband because my mother, who was getting on in years and a bit frail, could not care for my mentally retarded sister and me at the same time.

I grew up poor but safe. Surrounded by loving family members, I did not lack for emotional nurturing, but I hated being poor. Even at a young age I dreamed of the day when I could have the things that other people had (like a toilet inside the house!)

Raised Catholic, I saw God as merely a ritual or someone you prayed to when you were in trouble. After graduating from high school, I stopped going to church completely and pursued a college education. My only goal was money.

Three weeks after graduating from college, I moved to Florida with my best friend, where I began my pursuit to be a millionaire.

I bought into the American lie. That lie says, "Work as hard as you can, make as much money as you can, and he who dies with the most wins."

I got a job selling life insurance in Miami and soon got married. Unfortunately, my all-consuming passion was not my wife. Since my heart, my thoughts, and my manhood were all wrapped up in trying to get ahead and make money, I became known as a hard, selfish, and unforgiving guy.

After the birth of our daughter, my wife didn't go back to work, and we soon found ourselves in terrible debt. That just made me more determined to work harder to get us out of debt. It took five years, and by then I was the top agent at a large insurance company. By the time I hit forty, I was worth more than two million dollars. I had twenty-eight people working for me. I owned a large house on the water, a couple of boats, and, of course, his and her Mercedes in the garage.

I had met my goal.

One day I found out that my coworker and friend, Chuck, had cheated me out of some business. I was pretty sore because I always stuck up for him and had sent a lot of business his way over the years. I decided to let it go, or at least on the surface it looked like I had let it go. While I was opening another office for the company in

Boca Raton, Chuck had gotten promoted to district general manager. Now he signed my checks, and even though I harbored resentment on the inside, there was nothing I could do about it on the outside.

Three years later, he cheated me again.

I developed such an intense, all-consuming hatred of Chuck that I left my management position in the company and forged out on my own. Although I was not aware of it at the time, my hate was turning me into a negative, bitter person. My life began to fall apart. I lost 70% of my fortune, my big house, luxury boats, and fancy cars.

One day, while I was on a fishing trip in Alaska, I started having chest pains. Not caring much for doctors, I ignored the pain. Two months later, I experienced more chest pains. This time, I went to a doctor friend who rushed me to a cardiac hospital in Florida.

I had a heart catheterization, and they found six clogged arteries. Since my dad lived to be 93 years old, I never figured I would have a heart problem, but, as they did the angioplasty, I really started thinking I might die, and my biggest question was whether I was going to go to heaven. I thought I was a good person, but I wasn't sure that was enough. I knew God had been speaking to me throughout my life, but I had never listened. Now, God was asking for my undivided attention.

I left the hospital and decided to change my lifestyle. I quit smoking, bought a treadmill, and began eating healthy foods. It was still probable that I would have to have open-heart surgery. Not particularly happy about the prospect, I heard of a doctor in Houston who had devised a program to treat heart disease without surgery. He told me he could reverse my heart disease if I did exactly what he told me to do. A part of his orders addressed the physical, but another part had to do with my emotional and spiritual states. What I had discovered was that my diet and lack of exercise had poisoned my heart physically, but my bitterness and hatred toward Chuck had poisoned it spiritually.

The years of striving for wealth followed by the years of being consumed with resentment had taken a toll on my life. My marriage had suffered the most, and two years after my angioplasty, my wife and I decided to divorce.

One evening I was at the golf course bar and I met a guy who was a golf pro. He invited me to a prayer meeting at the home of another professional golfer. Still wondering whether I was going to heaven when I died made me kind of interested in attending the prayer meeting.

I walked into this multimillion-dollar home and saw about 80 people congregated in the living room. The chaplain for the PGA started speaking about the Big Bang and how it contradicts the Bible. I didn't care about that - I was miserable from the bitterness over Chuck, my bout with heart disease, the loss of my fortune, and the loss of my wife. About twenty minutes into the chaplain's talk, I raised my hand and asked him how to have the faith to meet God and have a relationship with Him. The chaplain ignored my question! At first I was embarrassed, but there was a voice inside me telling me I was asking the right question.

When I got up to leave, the pro golfer's wife pulled me aside and apologized to me. Then a pro football player came up to me and told me to buy the book, *Halftime*, a testimonial by a man named Bob Buford. I bought the book and started to read it.

One night while I was reading the book, I looked at the phone, picked it up, and called Chuck. I asked him if we could meet for breakfast and warned him that I was probably going to get a lot more out of the breakfast than he would.

I met him the next morning. I told Chuck about the hate and resentment that had consumed me for six years, I started to cry, and then I asked for his forgiveness. At that point, Chuck started to cry too. Both of us hugged when we left the restaurant.

That moment changed my life.

Not long after, my daughter and her friend invited me to church with them. I went, and the pastor talked about the lies that men buy into regarding success and that the only true success was to know God and have a relationship with Him. I knew right away that God was speaking to me. I went forward and asked God into my life.

God finally had my full attention. I got involved with the divorce care ministry at my church and also served as an usher.

A few years later, I got into an accident on my bicycle while I was training for a triathlon. I hit a rock and tumbled over my bike onto the ground. I got up, put the chain back on the bike, and rode home. Later, while I was taking a shower, I noticed a little swelling near my appendix, but I didn't think too much about it.

My daughter called to see if I wanted to go to dinner, so I told her I would come and pick her up at her mom's house. On my way to get her, I made a turn in the car and passed out. When I came to, I saw people surrounding my car and tapping on the window. Smoke filled the inside of the car. I got out of the car and groggily walked to the waiting ambulance. I called my daughter and told her I was going to the hospital.

I passed out again en route to the hospital. In the emergency room, I heard the doctors say, "Tilt the gurney, I think we are going to lose him this time." Once again, on the gurney, just like six years before during my angioplasty, I had the thought, "Am I going to go to heaven?" This time, however, I had a clear answer, "Yes, I am, I know the Lord." God, in all His mercy, healed my heart that day and gave me a peace that one day I would be with Him in heaven.

Recently, God has blessed me with the best business year ever. I am enjoying life - not through material possessions - but by knowing God and reaching out to others with the same message of hope and love that He used to rescue me from the bitterness that nearly choked my life.

"Then Peter came to Jesus and asked,
'Lord, how many times shall I forgive my
brother when he sins against me? Up to seven
times?'" Jesus answered, "I tell you not seven
times, but seventy-seven times."
Matthew 18:21-22

THINK ABOUT THIS

We hear a story like this and think we're not anything like Robert. Bitterness hasn't consumed us or affected our health. Yet, remember the title of his story, "Weeds of Bitterness." A weed starts as a microscopic seed under the earth. When it pops up, you wonder where in the world it came from. You didn't plant it or encourage it to grow. It seemed to just appear out of nowhere.

That's what bitterness and negative feelings do in our lives. We all have times in our life when we've been burned. It always hurts. First, we blame ourselves, but self-preservation quickly has us blaming others.

Even when we get into a conflict with another person, and we know we're right, we still need to let that person know that we're sorry for the misunderstanding. We need to pursue peace. We don't always need to fix it, and we don't always need to be right. We just need to be sorry that it happened and willing to forgive, forget, and move on.

QUESTIONS WE SHOULD ASK

Have you been the victim of someone else's bad behavior? How did
you react?

Is there someone you need to forgive or someone you need to ask to
forgive you?

What will happen to you when you die?

Appendix...

Bitterness, Forgiveness, Salvation

twelve

D E B B I E ' S   S T O R Y

Through the Eyes of a Child

*"The more I tried to wake her up, the stranger
her behavior became. She started walking into walls.
After I called the doctor again, I went back to her room
and saw her curled up in a fetal position.
Her eyes were rolled back into her head,
and her mouth was filled with foam."*

Many people, places, and things influenced me in my childhood. I was raised with a variety of different church affiliations - Episcopal, Dutch Reformed, Methodist, Baptist, Presbyterian, and Lutheran – but the greatest influence on my heart came from my mother who always told us to "love one another."

My father had a different type of influence on me. An alcoholic throughout my childhood, he often ignored me, leaving me feeling unwanted and alone.

Then there was my grandmother. I spent weekends with her in New

York City and always enjoyed her company. Bibles were everywhere in her apartment, and I could just tell that she loved God. In fact, years later, I would discover why I grew up knowing one particular Bible verse more than any other. The Bible my grandmother handed down to me as a baby had a note attached to the front cover that read: "Debbie, I always want you to remember my favorite verse - Philippians 4:13," but I forgot it.

I was a real rebel in my teenage years. At sixteen, I went to a Christian summer camp where I had a friend send drugs to me in the mail, and yet, at the same time, I was struck by the message of God's love that I heard there. I asked Jesus to come into my heart that summer, and I spent many hours writing and reflecting on my newfound relationship with Him.

After camp, the world awaited me, and I would have to make a choice as to which path of faith I would follow.

I ended up getting involved with the wrong group of people. Seemingly harmless looking on the outside, The Way was a Christian cult that was popular in the late 1960s and early 1970s. Known as "Jesus Freaks," they read the Bible, but also did drugs and encouraged its members to stay away from their families and friends. After two challenging years with them, I left the cult and went to college.

In college I decided to turn my back on God and manage my life in my own way on my own terms. Also by this time, I really felt mad at God. I had experienced the death of my boyfriend, a continual drug habit, and a few abortions.

After college I blended into the New York lifestyle. I had a successful career as an advertising director for a major bookstore chain, went club hopping, and was a social drug and alcohol user.

I was in the midst of the New York City drug scene when I met my soon-to-be husband. Eventually he got sober, and I started attending Al-Anon, a support group for loved ones of recovering alcoholics.

Together, we decided to move to Florida where we married a year later.

I continued to attend Al-Anon meetings in Florida. One night, I met a woman whose son was involved in a cult. I shared my own cult experiences with this woman, hoping to encourage her. The woman said to me, "You know, God was really talking to you tonight. You need to return to Him." I was shocked, yet I knew she was telling me the truth.

The truth was that God had not turned His back on me like I had thought. I started attending church, but I was looking for something more than the ritual of just going to church.

While I was pregnant with my first child, my father died of cancer. Two years later, my second child was born, and I was also taking care of my stepson, so I had three children to look after. I was pregnant, nursing, and also helping my husband in the family business. I was busy, to say the least.

When my first child turned three, I enrolled her in a Lutheran pre-school. The church would end up playing a key role in my spiritual journey.

The more I helped my husband in his business, the more we were able to accumulate nice things, including buying our first house, yet I was getting more frustrated by the day because I was carrying such a heavy load - caring for the children, managing the home, and helping him.

I was often torn between my home and the business. Then my husband started having problems with the business and put pressure on me to spend more time working rather than being at home. The result was a mountain of anger and resentment between us.

I was at a point where I needed something, but I didn't know what it was. I was sad all the time. I was angry and short-tempered with just about everyone, especially my husband. I was trying to satisfy everybody else, and I wasn't satisfied at all.

I held my "pew" space in church, but my spiritual life never seemed to go beyond that.

Then I started going to the Lutheran church where my daughter went to pre-school. There I was more than just a "bench warmer." I began to feel a hunger for God. My heart was being touched, and I desperately wanted the peace that others seemed to have, but something kept deterring my peace. I longed for my husband to join me at church instead of working or playing golf on Sunday mornings.

My husband's business problems increased, and he became more and more hostile and distant. Then I faced a new challenge with my daughter. When she was in kindergarten, she would fade out at night and go into a blank stare. Sometimes she would come into our bedroom, but not respond when I addressed her. My husband and I usually shrugged it off, assuming she was sleepwalking.

One night my daughter was in a dazed state when she started throwing up. I tried to wake her up, but she didn't respond. I called the doctor who told me I had to try to wake her up so she wouldn't choke. The more I tried to wake her up, the stranger her behavior became. She started walking into walls. After I called the doctor again, I went back to her room and saw her curled up in a fetal position. Her eyes were rolled back into her head, and her mouth was filled with foam.

The doctor told me to get her to the emergency room right away. As I carried her, I noticed her body becoming stiff. I kept talking to her, I prayed and sang, but still she wouldn't wake up.

In the ER several doctors and nurses immediately started jabbing needles into her and hooking her up to monitors. When the doctors stuck a tube down her throat, I noticed a tear rolling down her cheek.

I was terrified that she was going to die. I called my husband, who was away on a business trip and told him to come home. I hung up and paced back and forth, back and forth. I was scared, alone, and hopeless. Then I started praying.

The doctors finally moved my little girl to intensive care and diagnosed her as having had a grand mal seizure caused by a form of epilepsy. She was put on medication and three days later allowed to go home.

My husband came home from his trip, and the next day we were both awakened to strange noises. We soon realized that the noise we were hearing was the sound of our car being repossessed. That was the beginning of the end of our family business.

While I attended to the needs of our daughter, my husband sank into a severe depression. Life was becoming increasingly unbearable.

Within a month, my daughter started developing what looked like a rash on her body. A couple of days later, she broke out in a fever that climbed to 105 degrees. Dehydration set in, and the rash that now covered her entire body started to turn into sores everywhere, including the inside of her mouth.

The doctors diagnosed her with Stephen Johnson's Syndrome, a rare reaction to the seizure medication. I was told that nine out of ten people do not survive this syndrome. I was so frightened, but the most difficult thing to handle was watching my child suffer. She was in constant pain from the sores. I would swab the inside of her mouth every ten minutes. Her skin was purple and swollen, and she was totally disfigured.

The doctors informed me that if the sores progressed down her throat and into her heart, she would die. At that point, the sores had reached her throat.

I was getting to the point where I didn't think I could take any more of the pressure. I would look at her little body (she was only six at that time) and just cry. I really didn't understand why God would allow this sweet child to experience so much agony. One day, sitting in the hospital room, looking at my little girl, I broke down again. I cried out to God in anguish and bent over my daughter sobbing. Just then, she opened her eyes and looked at me and said, "Mom, don't worry. God will take care of me just fine. You just have to have faith."

God had just spoken to me through my six-year-old daughter! That was the turning point.

Within a couple of days, the sores stopped spreading, and her body healed. She never had another seizure again.

Today my daughter is a fifteen-year-old committed Christian who tells others in our community about her faith in God. As for me, I began attending a Bible-teaching church after my daughter's healing, and my husband came to know God as well. We are serving the Lord in different ways, but most of all we just want people to know how powerful He is and how He can change any life.

Never underestimate the power of God to reach people. In my case, it took many years and a little six-year-old girl's faith for me to hear God's voice.

Anything is possible with God.

"But seek first the kingdom of God and His righteousness, and all these things shall be added to you. Therefore do not worry about tomorrow, for tomorrow will worry about its own things. Sufficient for the day is its own trouble."
Matthew 6:33-34

THINK ABOUT THIS

The faith of a child is so precious. Children will believe anything you tell them. "A big man in a red suit comes down our chimney ... a little fairy brings you money when you put your tooth under your pillow ... a giant rabbit hides eggs for you to find..." The faith of a child is truly amazing.

The reality is that little children put their faith in the person they love. They believe and trust their parents unconditionally. That's what God wants from His children. "Just believe," God says over and over in the Bible. "Trust Me," He pleads with mankind.

God is faithful, and everything He tells us in the Bible is true. No one has ever been able to prove it's not. The question is: Do you have the faith to believe it?

QUESTIONS WE SHOULD ASK

Have you ever read the Bible? Do you believe it is God's Word?

What do you do when you feel like you can't take it anymore?

What lessons have you recently learned through a child?

Appendix. . .

Bible, Guidance, Faith

thirteen

V I C T O R ' S   S T O R Y

Hearing God's Voice in a Hurricane

*"Three months into her pregnancy, Ginny and I
got married. I was very nervous thinking that
we would all eventually contract AIDS.
I honestly didn't believe there was any hope for us."*

I had been divorced for years when I started to feel guilt over what I had done. My ex-wife and I met in college. Our relationship was volatile at best, and then it was torn apart by my unfaithfulness, but what plagued me the most was the fact that I had encouraged her to have an abortion.

My remorse led me to go back to my Catholic church to counsel with the priest regarding the matter. Though the priest concurred that I had committed a serious sin, he reassured me that God would forgive me if I repented.

I sought God's forgiveness, but soon went back to my old lifestyle.

I was a personal trainer, which meant there were always plenty of women who wanted to spend time with me. One day I met an attractive and vivacious woman at the gym named Ginny. My boss asked me to train her, and I gladly accepted the assignment. Ginny and I started spending a lot of time together. She was somebody that really liked to work out, like I did. Before long we were dating. We had so much in common. Our friendship connected us on a deep level, and then the relationship became more and more serious, but as it progressed, Ginny got nervous. She had a secret, and she knew she could no longer keep it from me. It was difficult because she really liked me and wanted the relationship to work, but she was afraid that if she told me, it would destroy what we had.

Ginny had always relied on relationships with men to fill the empty places in her heart. She got married in college and was divorced two years later. She struggled with unbearable loneliness, so she immediately pursued another relationship. Then she got immersed in the party scene and began to slip in and out of affairs. One particular man she had been dating ended up being HIV positive. He never told her. She actually found out she was infected when an insurance company turned her down.

Ginny broke off the relationship, moved back in with her parents, and tried to start over. She began to search for God and His comfort and protection. She said that it was the first time in her life she felt comfortable being by herself. That same man who infected her ended up dying a year and a half later. Ginny felt terrified that she would be next.

We met a year after his death. I was the first person she had dated since she found out she was HIV positive. As our relationship evolved, she knew the time had come to tell me. When she did tell me, my heart sank. I think what I wrestled with the most was the question, "If Ginny had diabetes or cancer, would I still want a relationship with her?" my answer was "yes." So I decided that just because she was HIV positive didn't mean we couldn't continue a relationship.

We stayed together and grew in our love for one another.

Throwing caution to the wind one night, we slept together, and Ginny got pregnant. When I found out she was pregnant, I thought about abortion. Even after everything I had gone through with my ex-wife's abortion – the guilt and the regret – I still saw abortion as the only means of escape. I was convinced that all of us would die; we would be HIV positive and we would die from AIDS, all three of us. Then I felt God really spoke to me loud and clear that if I killed this baby, He would take my life. It was overwhelming. I really didn't know God, but I certainly knew I had to do the right thing.

Three months into her pregnancy, Ginny and I got married. I was very nervous thinking that we would all eventually contract AIDS. I honestly didn't believe there was any hope for us. I thought for sure I was going to have another divorce on my hands and possibly the AIDS virus too. I just didn't see how it could work.

Our son, Gino, was born on July 14, 1993, and our second son, Emilio, was born fifteen months later. We were told that when our sons turned two, we would have to test them for HIV. I recognized from the beginning that we needed help, so I sought the best help I could – God. We started going to a local Catholic church. All Ginny would do when we went to church was cry. She really struggled with all the guilt. It was so severe that at first she dreaded going to the services.

After a short time at a Catholic church, we tried a Baptist church. Then we were invited to another church that was very charismatic and focused on healing and prosperity.

We were genuinely seeking God. We knew that God was the answer, but quite honestly, we really wanted God to fit into our plan, not the other way around. Eventually we ended up at a great Bible-believing church and started understanding that God's plans were better than ours.

Finally, when our youngest son turned two and a half, Ginny and I had them both tested for the HIV virus. We had to wait two weeks to get the results back. That was brutal. It was around Christmas time, and we were really trying to focus on the Lord and celebrate, but, deep down inside, we couldn't stop thinking about the "what ifs."

The doctor finally called, and, in a very sterile and cold voice, let us know that the test results were in, and we needed to come to the office. I remember trying to figure out what the tests results were by her voice, but it was detached and so matter-of-fact that I couldn't tell. It was all very upsetting.

Ginny and I waited in anxiety for the doctor's appointment. As we walked into the doctor's office, she immediately let us know that the tests came back negative!

It was a miracle. Ginny had vaginal births and breast-fed both of our sons, and yet they tested negative to the virus. They never have to be tested again, unless they are exposed to the virus by another means. It was a huge, huge relief.

God had protected my children – the very children that I thought were doomed to die.

Though Ginny has been infected with the HIV virus since 1991, she has not been sick or experienced full-blown AIDS, nor has she had to take medication. She does get tested for her immune count every three months, but so far so good. I go for testing every six months, and to date I have never tested positive.

By the way, Ginny and I wanted to expand our family one more time. Rather quickly, she became pregnant. This time however, the doctors recommended that she take the HIV "meds" during the pregnancy to help ensure that the baby would not have the virus. We sought the Lord every step of the way, and He answered us each time. As we prayed about the medication, it became very clear what to do. Ginny had opened up my Bible to Ezekiel 33:4-5, which reads: "...then whoever hears the sound of the trumpet and does not take warning, if the sword comes and takes him away, his blood shall be on his own head. He heard the sound of the trumpet, but did not take warning; his blood shall be upon himself. But he who takes warning will save his life." Ginny went on the "meds" when she was five months pregnant.

Four months later, Maria Grace was born, tested negative for the HIV virus four times, and will never have to be tested again!

God has worked miracles in our lives. We now have three beautiful, healthy children and are enjoying our life as a family. I still test negative for the HIV virus, and Ginny is training for her first post-children triathlon.

Two broken people with a history of broken relationships have built a loving and successful marriage through God's mercy and grace. What seemed impossible so many years ago – to have a family – has been made possible through the powerful hand of God.

"Then you will call upon Me and go and pray to Me,
and I will listen to you. And you will seek Me and find Me,
when you search for Me with all your heart. I will be found by you, says
the LORD, and I will bring you back from your captivity; I will gather
you from all the nations and from all the places where I have driven you,
says the LORD, and I will bring you to the place
from which I cause you to be carried away captive."
Jeremiah 29:12-14

THINK ABOUT THIS

How often do we seek God hoping that He will fit into our plans? We all think we know what's best for our own life. When we hit a curve in our road, we believe we can figure it all out if we just had the resources to do it.

To see your life through God's perspective would be a real eye opener. The things you think are so important today would probably change rather quickly. The things you tend to put aside would probably be the ones that mean the most in the long run.

The Bible says, "And do not be conformed to this world, but be transformed by the renewing of your mind, that you may prove what is that good and acceptable and perfect will of God" (Romans 12:2). If you want God's will for your life, you have to begin by renewing your mind. It doesn't come naturally to think or see from God's perspective. The only way to learn to think like God is to spend time in God's Word reading what He thinks. Read the Bible. It's such a simple answer to many complex questions, but it's the only answer.

QUESTIONS WE SHOULD ASK

Do you know what God's will for your life is? Write it down.

What is something from your past that you felt guilty about? How did you deal with it?

Are you facing a hopeless situation? Think of two things you can do that would help you find hope for tomorrow?

Appendix . . .

Seeking God's Will, Guilt, Hope

fourteen

E M I L Y ' S   S T O R Y

Putting the Ball in God's Court

"They told me I should just 'speak' the cancer away, and if I had enough faith, I would be healed. This just didn't seem right to me, and I became confused and angry."

I had no use for religion. I saw it as something that involved ritual and tradition. As an engineer, this just did not fit in with my analytical mind.

I was experiencing serious financial troubles and setbacks. All the number crunching and juggling of finances never seemed to help me get ahead. I could not see a way out of my financial problems.

One day, I had had it. I looked up, and with a somewhat angry challenge, I said, "All right, God, if You are really there, then prove it to me."

Suddenly, a bizarre series of events started to take place in my life.

I was temporarily relocated to a special job, building a nuclear plant in Soddy Daisy, Tennessee. I worked long hours and made a lot of money. Living in Soddy Daisy, there was virtually nothing to do, so I was also able to save a great deal of money.

Then there were the little things that brought money my way - the bank error in my favor, the rebate check in the mail, and the old Navy pea coat I forgot about that had money in the pocket.

At first I felt like I was in a different dimension. It was all just too good to be true. Then it became clear to me - there must be a God up there after all.

I knew I had thrown out that angry challenge to God to prove Himself, but I never expected Him to answer me...at least not so quickly. The question now was: "Who is this God and how do I talk to Him?"

I called my sister because I knew she had been reading the Bible for years.

"Tell me about God," I asked her. She said, "Okay, what do you want to know?" I asked her how I could get to know Him. She asked me if I had a Bible (which I didn't), and then she said she would send one to me right away.

After work the following Friday, I got back to my hotel and found a postal slip. It was the package from my sister.

I got back in the car and rushed to the post office. However, by the time I arrived, it was closed. I couldn't believe it. Now it would be a whole weekend before I could get the Bible I was waiting for.

When I walked into the room, I threw my purse on the bed and noticed an opened Bible on the bedside table. I walked over to it and saw that it was open to the Gospel of Mark. Although I had been staying in this hotel for some time, I had never noticed a Bible on the table before.

My sister had said to start by reading the Gospels, beginning with Matthew. She had to tell me it was two-thirds of the way through the book. I began to read. Many questions came to mind, but I couldn't stop reading. Each afternoon, as soon as my workday was over, I rushed back to the hotel to read.

Then I became curious as to what God might do for me, if I only asked Him. After all, when I needed money, He had provided.

In little ways, I would seek His help. When I couldn't find something, I'd ask God, and I'd find it. I needed a parking space at the mall, I'd ask God, and I'd find one right next to the handicapped space.

I started wondering if there was a catch to the "God" thing. After all, He was giving me everything that I asked for. There must be something that I had to do in return.

I called up my sister and said, "Now what do I do?" I told her that I kept asking God for things and He kept giving them to me. In my world there was no such thing as a free lunch, so I needed to know what my part was in this whole deal.

I'll never forget my sister's answer. She told me I just had to love Him. I told her again there must be something more that I had to do, and she repeated, "Just love God." At that point I felt like my sister was not being straight with me, and I got frustrated and pretty upset. She encouraged me to keep reading and told me I would soon understand.

I opened my Bible and continued to read. When I got to John 3:16, I sat back stunned. It said, "For God so loved the world that He gave His only begotten Son, that whoever believes in Him should not perish but have everlasting life." Then it hit me. All God did want from me was my love!

Three years later, I faced my first big challenge. After a routine exam at the doctor, I was told that my pap smear had come back showing the possibility of cancer. A biopsy revealed that it was, in fact, malignant. When the doctors performed the surgery to remove the cancer, they found a great deal more. A week later I was told that I had a second cancer, a rare and aggressive strain. The doctors wanted me to have a radical hysterectomy. I was only twenty-seven years old with no children. The thought of it was overwhelming.

The group of women that I went to Bible study with believed I didn't need to have surgery. They told me I should just "speak" the cancer away, and if I had enough faith, I would be healed. This just didn't seem right to me, and I became confused and angry. My friends were telling me that either I did not have enough faith or there was sin in my life. I knew that I did not have enough faith; in fact, I could never have enough faith. As far as sin went, well, I was certain I would always be a sinner, but wasn't that why Jesus died on the cross for me? What my friends were saying did not fit with what I knew of God.

I had the hysterectomy. While in recovery, my friends came to my room and told me that I could still have children - that is, if I had enough faith. I remember just lying in my bed thinking that these people were nuts. I had about all I could take from them. It was hard enough to have a hysterectomy, but to have the added pressure of guilt was really more than I wanted to hear. God sustained me and reassured me that He was not applying the pressure or the guilt.

Two weeks later my father died. I felt like I had been whacked in the head. I questioned God, but I knew that God had made me a tough cookie - tough enough to handle this trial. The Bible said so. I read it in 1 Corinthians 10:13: "No temptation has overtaken you except such as is common to man; but God is faithful, who will not allow you to be tempted beyond what you are able, but with the temptation will also make the way of escape, that you may be able to bear it."

A couple of years later I found a lump in my throat. It was diagnosed as a cancerous tumor on my thyroid. Once again I faced surgery. Fortunately, the doctors were able to get the entire tumor and leave enough of my thyroid so that I did not have to take medication.

Over the next five years, I experienced two more bouts with cancer and two more surgeries – one on my skull and one on my face, and I'm still here to talk about it seven years later.

If you asked me today, I would say that I have a chest full of medals, and I wear them proudly. They're not colorful ribbons or silver or gold, but scars. I've been a soldier in the war called cancer, and I've been decorated with medals I didn't earn. I'm proud that God gave me His strength. So, when I feel pain, I remember what He did and then consider it a privilege to suffer a bit as He did.

I realize now that tragedies will occur in my life and my body will fall apart. I also know the difference God can make in my life if I will allow Him to walk through the hard times with me.

"In this you greatly rejoice, though now for a little while, if need be, you have been grieved by various trials, that the genuineness of your faith, being much more precious than gold that perishes, though it is tested by fire, may be found to praise, honor, and glory at the revelation of Jesus Christ."
1 Peter 1:6-7

THINK ABOUT THIS

It's an outrageous thing to challenge God to prove Himself, and yet most of us do just that. However, that is a form of communication with God, and, in one sense, a form of prayer. We need to learn how to talk to God and how to listen to God. Obviously, friends don't have all the answers, just as Emily's friends were no help in her greatest time of need.

Sometimes we face things in life that bring us up short. God, however, is not surprised. In fact, He saw it all from the beginning. He will always give us His strength to meet every situation, small or large, ordinary or extraordinary.

The Bible says, "Ask and it will be given to you; seek and you will find; knock and the door will be opened to you" (Luke 11:9). There will be times when life seems unbearable, but if you seek God in the midst of the trial you are going through, you will find Him.

QUESTIONS WE SHOULD ASK

Are you facing major problems and wondering if God even cares? Think of one need in your life and ask God to meet that need.

Have others given you advice that makes you question God? Write down one bit of bad advice you were given and see if it lines up with God's Word.

Do you suffer in some way physically or emotionally? Ask God to ease your pain.

Appendix . . .

Finances, Providence of God, Suffering

fifteen

TONY'S STORY

A Family of Crime

"Lying on the floor, covered in my own blood,
I winced as he put his gun in my mouth and said,
'You cross me, and I'll kill you.'"

I was born in Brooklyn to an Italian Catholic father and a Jewish mother. When I was quite young, I moved to Queens to a subdivision that was ruled by the mob. I was the kind of kid that needed structure in my life, and unfortunately I didn't get it from my parents. They were involved in the hippie movement - far from conventional or structured. My dad worked in the recording industry, and my parents were heavily involved in the social phenomenon of drugs, free sex (including swinging), and rock 'n roll.

Although my parents were kind, they were not exactly the kind of people who would sacrifice their lives for their kids. They lived a very indulgent lifestyle, and parameters, rules, and tending after kids were not a part of it.

In our neighborhood, kids went in three different directions. They could turn to drugs, turn to organized crime, or (if they were very fortunate) go to college. Most of us turned to organized crime, and for a very good reason. The crime family offered for many of us a place where we could belong. We looked up to those involved in the mob because they had the power, the money, the nice things, and the women.

Working on the streets for "the family" taught me to be unemotional, hard, and cold. As a teenager, my job was to collect envelopes of cash from drug dealers and derelicts and deliver them to my boss. If they didn't cooperate, they would get hurt. You have to be pretty hard and cold to do that job.

I did it well, so well that when I turned seventeen, I started working for the mob full-time. I became fairly successful in my new position and in my relations with my new family. I had money and women and respect in my neighborhood.

My parents spent a great deal of their time at a nudist camp, so I had been introduced to sexuality at a very early age. They took me to camp with them for the first time when I was thirteen. Imagine entering puberty and being introduced to sexual feelings and acts at a nudist camp! Deep down I was angry with my parents and vented this anger through violence. And, of course, organized crime is all about violence.

Anger was not the only thing I had to deal with. Paranoia was a given in working for the mob, and I had a surplus of it. Although this trait kept me alive on the streets, it debilitates human emotions and relationships.

By the time I was twenty-five, I excelled at organized crime. I worked as a bodyguard, served as a thug, and was considered a top gopher by the older statesmen of the "family." Although I did many bad things, I knew I would not be a "career" man as many of them were. Somewhere deep down I always knew this was not what I should be doing. I had no desire to be a mobster for the rest of my life. Although I blew God off time and time again, I also knew God was trying to reach me.

The turning point in my life came on one very frightening night.

It started with this leather warehouse. My friend, who was a good thief, robbed the warehouse. He had $35,000 worth of goods he wanted to sell me. I set up a deal with someone to buy the goods for $50,000. That gave me a $15,000 profit, which was pretty good.

It was not good for the mob, and they wanted to make sure I understood that. When the head of the family came to my door, I knew that there was a very real possibility I would be dead in a matter of minutes. When his men chased my girlfriend away and had me put on some music, everything became suddenly very real to me. This was the result of a messed up life, and it would probably be my death. He pulled out his gun and struck me over the head. I fell to the ground, and then he pistol-whipped me. Lying on the floor, covered in my own blood, I winced as he put his gun in my mouth and said, "You cross me, and I'll kill you."

I remember looking at my hand and seeing blood. There was blood everywhere - on the carpet, the couch, even the drapes.

The mob is always one step ahead of you. They knew I would try to escape, and, as is their fashion, they threatened that if I were to double-cross them, they would come after my parents, my girlfriend, and anyone else related to me.

My back was to the wall and I sought God's help. After going to the hospital, I went to my Catholic church and asked the priest to baptize me so if I died I would not go to hell. The only thing the priest could do was bless me, but it planted a seed in my heart - one that would take root much later.

The mob had a plan. They wanted me to be part of a scheme to get back at the leather warehouse. They assured me that I would come through it and be sipping Pina Coladas soon on a beach in the

Caribbean, but I knew better. It was a death trap.

All of this was of God. I believe God was saying, "I've had enough. This is not My plan for your life. I want you out of all this completely."

So I packed my bags and headed out of town. I went by to see my mother, then moved to another state and tried to turn over a new leaf. I began going to a Catholic church regularly and saying my prayers. Before long, however, I was involved with a band and started touring and performing at various clubs. Though no longer involved in organized crime, I was still fighting the demons within. Alcohol, promiscuity, and anger had not loosened their hold on my life. Time and again I promised God I would change my life, but time after time I broke those promises.

After a stint performing with the band, I started a reptile business. I became very successful importing reptiles from all over the world. I had more than fifteen employees, and two of them turned out to have a large influence on my life. They were Christian men, and they really loved Jesus. We became good friends. They kept telling me about God's forgiveness and God's love. I had never believed that I could be forgiven for the things I had done.

After a while I started getting into illegal importing of exotic animals and endangered species. Eventually I met a girl named Carla and moved in with her. We had two kids within three years, but I was cheating on her repeatedly. God used my two friends to relay His love and forgiveness toward me, but He also used them to warn me of the consequences of my sinful lifestyle.

Although I had many sins that I struggled with, my overwhelming problem was pride and arrogance, and God knew that.

He started by working on Carla's heart. She began attending a Bible-teaching church, and I would sometimes go with her. Six months into the pregnancy of our third child, we got married. I noticed changes taking place in my wife's life, but I was still struggling with whether God could forgive me, and I was still living an immoral lifestyle.

About a year later, Federal Marshals came to my business with guns drawn, seizing more than nineteen boxes of paperwork and receipts. I felt the same doom I'd felt the night the mob showed up at my door.

The department of U.S. Fish and Wildlife (part of the USDA) had a huge file on me, and a jail sentence was pending. I had finally come to the end of myself.

Up in our bedroom, I put my head in Carla's lap and started to cry. I was so sorry for all the bad things I had brought into her life and the lives of our children. She was loving, comforting, and gentle with me. I was a broken man, and I needed a Savior. I just wanted to start over and live my life in God's love and for God. It was a major turning point in my life. That day I surrendered my life to Christ.

Some things changed overnight. I stopped cussing, had a different attitude and outlook on life, and was far more humble and personable. I also got involved with our church and began to read the Bible, but sin has its consequences, and two years later my court case came up, and I was given a sentence of one year and a day in prison.

Things at home were also heating up. Just five weeks before going to prison, Carla and I both took off our wedding rings and were pretty sure it was time to call it quits. Even so, we decided to start counseling two to three times a week. By the week before I left for prison, I looked over at my wife lying in bed and realized she was everything I had ever wanted. God had really changed my heart, and He had changed hers as well.

I served out my prison term. In the midst of it, God continued to work in my heart. One particular incident involved my five-year-old daughter. I had been in prison about three or four months and, as I always called my wife twice a day, I called and talked to my daughter. She said, "Daddy, I don't want you to go to school anymore. I want you to come home for a couple of minutes." The kids thought I was in school, not prison. But it was the "couple of minutes" that got me. When she was very little, she would always ask me to come and lie down with her for a couple of minutes until she fell asleep. She then said, "Daddy, I don't understand why God would take you away and not bring you back for a couple of minutes. I'm praying that God will bring my daddy home, even for a couple of minutes." She broke my heart.

The next morning I woke up and called my wife. She was excited and told me that something wonderful had happened the night before. My daughter came on the phone and began to tell me about a dream she had. "Daddy," she said, "before I went to bed last night, I asked God to bring you home for a couple of minutes. Then I had this dream that you were laying next to me. Oh, Daddy, God did bring you home for a couple of minutes." She was so excited and happy. I knew God had answered the prayers of a five-year old. I realized that even when I was stuck in prison, God was still God, and He could take care of my family and me.

Looking back, I see that all through my life, God was intervening, even during the times when I did not acknowledge Him.

Today I own a pet store, I'm active in my church, and I love being a husband and father. However, my greatest joy is my relationship with God.

Only God can meet someone in a pit and bring him out. That's what God did for me, and that's what He will do for you!

"The LORD says, 'I will give you back what you lost to the stripping locusts, the cutting locusts, the swarming locusts, and the hopping locusts. It was I who sent this great destroying army against you. Once again you will have all the food you want, and you will praise the LORD your God, who does these miracles for you.'"
Joel 2:25-26

THINK ABOUT THIS

Your life has been pushed to the wall, there is no way to escape, and the borrowed time that you have been living on is up! This was the way Tony lived his life. Why? As an outside observer, you can't help but read this story and think to yourself, "Thank goodness I am not in that guy's situation." Imagine having your life threatened, living on the run, no real family support, and in trouble with the law, all the while knowing that it will one day catch up to you.

Unfortunately, many of us do read this story and identify. In fact, some of us may be where Tony was a few years ago. Our lives are on the verge of destruction, and the very things we care about are slowly slipping from our grasp. The words, "Help me," are becoming all too familiar to our inner vocabulary. Tony tried over and over again to make it on his own. What was driving him on his path of self-destruction? He mentions anger, paranoia, a poor childhood, and pride. These are all symptoms of a life out of control, a life that has no direction or purpose. Tony desperately wanted to have a life of significance, but he initially chose to find that through crime and everything that came with it. He eventually found it in a personal, not religious, relationship with God. God gave him the family that he never had and was always seeking.

Life is short, and his daughter's words, "for a couple of minutes," seem to resonate in all of our hearts. Tony's daughter was deeply in love with her daddy and completely unaware of his life. Tony loved his family and came to realize that those "couple of minutes" are significant. In Tony's life, as in Debbie's story, a child's words changed everything. How about you? Are you willing to give God a "couple of minutes" and hear what He has to say? If God can love Tony with an everlasting love, God can love you.

QUESTIONS WE SHOULD ASK

What areas in your life do you feel are "out of control"? What can you do to change that?

Is pride keeping you from making those needed changes in your life?

Are you seeking that personal relationship with God? Take a "couple of minutes" and talk to God about your life.

Appendix . . .

Self Control, Pride, Salvation

sixteen

M E G A N ' S   S T O R Y

The Woman at the Well

So Jesus left the Judean countryside and went back to Galilee. To get there, he had to pass through Samaria. He came into Sychar, a Samaritan village that bordered the field Jacob had given his son Joseph. Jacob's well was still there. Jesus, worn out by the trip, sat down at the well. It was noon.

A woman, a Samaritan, came to draw water. Jesus said, "Would you give me a drink of water?" (His disciples had gone to the village to buy food for lunch.)

The Samaritan woman, taken aback, asked, "How come you, a Jew, are asking me, a Samaritan woman, for a drink?" (Jews in those days wouldn't be caught dead talking to Samaritans.)

Jesus answered, "If you knew the generosity of God and who I am, you would be asking me for a drink, and I would give you fresh, living water." The woman said, "Sir, you don't even have a bucket to draw with, and this well is deep. So how are you going to get this 'living water'?

Are you a better man than our ancestor Jacob, who dug this well and drank from it, he and his sons and livestock, and passed it down to us?"

Jesus said, "Everyone who drinks this water will get thirsty again and again. Anyone who drinks the water I give will never thirst-not ever. The water I give will be an artesian spring within, gushing fountains of endless life."

The woman said, "Sir, give me this water so I won't ever get thirsty, won't ever have to come back to this well again!"

He said, "Go call your husband and then come back."

"I have no husband," she said.

That's nicely put: 'I have no husband.' You've had five husbands, and the man you're living with now isn't even your husband. You spoke the truth there, sure enough."

"Oh, so you're a prophet! Well, tell me this: Our ancestors worshiped God at this mountain, but you Jews insist that Jerusalem is the only place for worship, right?"

"Believe me, woman, the time is coming when you Samaritans will worship the Father neither here at this mountain nor there in Jerusalem. You worship guessing in the dark; we Jews worship in the clear light of day. God's way of salvation is made available through the Jews. But the time is coming-it has, in fact, come-when what you're called will not matter and where you go to worship will not matter.

"It's who you are and the way you live that count before God. Your worship must engage your spirit in the pursuit of truth. That's the kind of people the Father is out looking for: those who are simply and honestly themselves before him in their worship. God is sheer being itself – Spirit. Those who worship him must do it out of their very being, their spirits, their true selves, in adoration."

The woman said, "I don't know about that. I do know that the Messiah is coming. When he arrives, we'll get the whole story."

"I am he," said Jesus. "You don't have to wait any longer or look any further."

Just then the disciples came back. They were shocked. They couldn't believe he was talking with that kind of a woman. No one said what they were all thinking, but their faces showed it.

The woman took the hint and left. In her confusion she left her water pot. Back in the village she told the people, "Come see a man who knew all about the things I did, who knows me inside and out. Do you think this could be the Messiah?" And they went out to see for themselves (The Message).
JOHN 4:4-30

"Once again I found myself divorced and decided that marriage, though instituted by God, really didn't work."

Have you ever craved love - that desire to have someone want you just as you are? Have you ever entertained a dream that Prince Charming would come and love and care for you forever? I did. Even as a child, I longed to be loved and to know that I was cherished and special.

My family was neither strange nor dysfunctional, but they were old school, firm, and without much affection. We moved to the States from Germany when I was two years old. When I became a teenager, I was affected by the sexual revolution. A sudden wave of sexual freedom for women swept through the country, and I was on the crest of its impact.

By age fourteen, I had lost my virginity, and by eighteen, I was pregnant. My boyfriend and I decided the only right thing to do was to get married.

Our marriage lasted three years before I filed for divorce. As a young single mom, my lifestyle was far from stable. I started drinking and spent most of my time in and out of relationships. Soon I was remarried, but my second marriage only lasted eight months before it too ended in divorce. At twenty-six, I was an alcoholic with two failed marriages.

Still seeking love, I continued to sleep around. I was successful in the workplace as well as in social settings, but my emotional state became more intense as my craving for love increased. At the same time, my anger and contempt for men were on the rise, and I always managed to see men as the problem, never me.

I met my third husband at the law firm where I worked. We immediately began sleeping together behind his secretary's back (who happened to be his girlfriend and with whom he was cheating on his wife). Because of me, he dumped his secretary, his wife dumped him, and after a respectable amount of time, we began living together. Seven years later, we were married. Eight months after the wedding, I left him for another man. Three months into this affair, I became disillusioned, and I wanted to return to my husband, but it was too late.

In my desperation to piece together a marriage I had already destroyed, I came to the end of my rope. It was August 6, 1982. I had a horrendous fight with my husband, slammed the phone down, and went screaming to my room. Because my young son was in the next room, I closed the door and then started throwing things against the walls and yelling uncontrollably. I was so exhausted from my outburst that I sat down on the edge of my bed. I was in deep pain because I kept making the same mistakes over and over, and I had just done it again. I wanted to kill myself, but I didn't want to die. I sat there holding a gun in my hand, and then I noticed the Bible I had purchased two weeks earlier. I looked at it and cried out, "God, if You are even out there, You can have my life. I don't want it anymore!"

It took three days to figure out something dramatic had happened. I was not the same, my outlook was different, the world seemed to have changed overnight.

That night in my bedroom, I had met God.

Eight months after this radical conversion, I met a man who had just moved to Florida from California. A gifted musician, he was a spiritual giant in our congregation that was made up of new Christians like myself. Within four months we were married. Finally, I would be able to experience marriage the way it was supposed to be! After all, we were both Christians.

A few months into our marriage, to my horror, I discovered that my new husband was physically abusive. I became his punching bag whenever things went wrong for him at work or at home. As the violence increased, I also found out that he was addicted to cocaine - an addiction he had been fighting for more than fifteen years. After four and a half years, he left me for one of his many girlfriends.

Once again I found myself divorced and decided that marriage, though instituted by God, really didn't work. It quickly became apparent that my attitude was not right. Although I still had a fear of marriage, God began working on my thoughts and ideas regarding the subject. Sarcastically, I would often tell the Lord that if He ever wanted me to marry again, the man would have to not only meet my list of requirements, but also have an unusual name!

I started attending a new church, and there I met GianPaolo. Five months later, he proposed. Throughout our courtship, God had been working on my heart and renewing my purity and innocence.

I still look back and remember my wedding night with him - I was embarrassed to get undressed! (How hilarious considering my promiscuous and lustful background), but in an awesome and miraculous way, as only God can, He had restored my sense of innocence.

Recently, GianPaolo and I celebrated our eleventh wedding anniversary. Together, we are faithfully serving on the staff at our church. God has been good to this "woman at the well." It's been nineteen years since I met God on that dire night in my bedroom. I can honestly say that He has restored my life and given me a new purpose, attitude, behavior, and sense of being.

In my promiscuous years of craving, I killed myself emotionally because I was seeking someone to love me, but God came into my life and gave me His perfect love and ended my search.

Just like the woman in the Bible who went to the well dry, broken, rejected, hopeless, and fearful and met her Savior Jesus, I have been given the dream of my childhood - a Man who will love me and make me complete. That Man is Jesus Christ.

He is waiting to meet you at the well of your misery and give you Living Water. Will you turn to Him and drink?

"They will be my people, and I will be their God. I will give them singleness of heart and action, so that they will always fear me for their own good and the good of their children after them. I will make an everlasting covenant with them: I will never stop doing good to them, and I will inspire them to fear me, so that they will never turn away from me. I will rejoice in doing them good and will assuredly plant them in this land with all my heart and soul."
Jeremiah 32:38-41

THINK ABOUT THIS

Megan was a woman desperately looking for love in a world that views love as an emotion and not a commitment. The men in her life were not the problem; it was her perspective. We tend to look at our relationships as a way to fulfill us, and when they don't, we walk away.

We need to look deep within ourselves and resolve the longing we feel for fulfillment. God put that longing there to draw us to Himself. He desires a relationship with us. It's hard to imagine why the God of the universe wants our love so much, but He is love, and therefore He will always love His creation. He also wants to use us to love a hurting world.

Just as Jesus used the woman at the well to reach the entire community of Samaria, He is also using Megan to reach women within her church. The Bible says that "God chose the foolish things of the world to shame the wise; God chose the weak things of the world to shame the strong" (1 Corinthians 1:27). Allow God to use you regardless of your past. You may be the foolish one He wants to use to confound the wise.

QUESTIONS WE SHOULD ASK

What are some misconceptions of marriage that you have had?

Have you been in an adulterous affair and need repentance and forgiveness? If you have walked through this type of valley, think of how God could use your pain to help others.

Have you experienced God's perfect love in your life? List three ways God has shown you His love recently.

Appendix . . .

Marriage, Adultery, Love of God

seventeen

G R A D Y ' S   S T O R Y

Living at the End of the Rope

"You would probably think this little boy came from a broken family, an impoverished neighborhood, had a horrific home life, or a learning disability. Not true.
I defied all these stereotypes."

Little boys should play games like cops and robbers or cowboys and Indians or even be immersed in video games, fire trucks, and bicycles. They should catch frogs, watch a trail of ants, and collect every bug they can find with wonder. But when a little boy gets immersed in alcohol and drugs instead of hanging out with other little boys, he finds himself isolated because he doesn't fit in. And if that same little boy becomes angry and frustrated, despairing of life itself - all before turning age twelve - well, what happens?

You would probably think this little boy came from a broken family, an impoverished neighborhood, had a horrific home life, or a learning disability. Not true. I defied all these stereotypes. In fact, my parents are still together. I grew up in a fairly affluent environment, lacking or wanting for nothing. My IQ was so high that I was put into gifted classes. I was good looking, and I had a strong and muscular build.

However, by the age of seven, I was smoking cigarettes, drinking hard liquor, and getting high on pot. I hung around my older sisters and their friends because they were popular. I wanted to fit in, but I never felt like I did, and I was willing to do anything to be popular.

My father was a schoolteacher, my mother a businesswoman, the chief of police a family friend, and both my sisters homecoming queens. I was pretty active in school and even performed on a local weekly television program called "Treasure Chest," but deep down something was wrong.

When I was seven and in the second grade, my mother pulled me out of public school and put me in a private Catholic school. I hated leaving my friends and hated my new school. Fear and anger festered and soon my only relief came from alcohol and drugs.

Along with being a child alcoholic and drug user, I also became a good liar. By the time I was eleven or twelve, I had overdosed twice. My father exhausted a million dollar insurance policy on me with psychologists and psychiatrists. He was always trying to find out what was wrong with me, but it never worked because I would just lie to all the counselors.

In the Catholic school, I was turned off by religion. The whole experience really pushed me away from God and religion. That's not to blame the Catholic system; it's just that I saw so much hypocrisy. I actually got in trouble once when I brought my Bible to school! It was a very ugly time for me. I hated the school and felt disdain for God as well.

Whenever I drank, smoked pot, or did drugs, I fit in. Then all the partying started to backfire and take its toll on me. By the time I was twelve, I had tried to commit suicide twice. I remember one time actually drinking gasoline to wash down some pills. I also had thoughts of killing my parents. I was raging inside – and it dominated my life.

When I was in the sixth grade, my parents enrolled me in a special drug program. I stuck with the program for about eight months and then called my mom one night and asked to come home. I stood in a phone booth on a street corner in Miami, Florida, and heard my mother tell me that I could not come home. I walked across the street, determined I would not go back to the clinic. As I walked, a man in a truck motioned to me. Distraught, I went over to the truck and got in. The man raped me. When he was done, he kicked me out of the truck. I just started walking and didn't tell a soul.

Eventually I went back home. However, after blowing myself up with gunpowder (I was drunk at the time), and seriously burning my face, my parents once again sought out a drug program for me. On the advice of the local police, at age thirteen, I started going to Narcotics Anonymous. I actually liked the program, and I stayed clean and sober for eight years, but I was still the same person - filled with anger, frustration, and lies.

On the outside, I looked okay because I was sober. Deep down, I still didn't care. I did, however, become motivated to earn money. I actually started my own tile business in the tenth grade. After high school, I got a job as a bouncer in a bar. It was then that I began drinking again and got back into substance abuse. Also, I discovered girls, sleeping with as many as I could.

Before long I was selling drugs. I lost my job and ended up homeless. My life consisted of doing odd jobs so I could survive and buy drugs. Then, instead of looking for odd jobs, I turned to robbery. I robbed everyone I knew, so much so that when I picked up a local phone book, I could not find a home I had not robbed! I again moved back home, but again got kicked out. I even spent time at the Salvation Army and got kicked out of there too. I went to jail on several occasions and liked it because it was warm and safe.

I was always battling demons inside me and suffering emotionally under the guilt and self-hatred that was eating away at me. I was angry at the world, God, and myself. Suicide for me was still a viable option.

As I continued to walk my wayward path, I got involved with a friend who ran a prostitution ring out of his home. He would drive the girls to their tricks and then rob homes while he was waiting. I remember feeling horrible every time I dropped a girl off to do her trick. One night I was standing on the porch of a crack house and asked God to let me die or help me because I didn't want to live this way anymore.

Two days later I was arrested. I was relieved and called my mom and told her I was in jail, but that I did not want to be bailed out. I finally felt safe.

I received a one-year sentence and was sent to the third worst maximum-security prison in Florida. While I was there, I met regularly with a counselor. One day when I was in her office, I noticed a book on her desk entitled, *The Search for Significance Through Jesus Christ*. I asked her if she was a Christian. She said, "Yes." I then asked her why Christianity hadn't worked for me. I had gone forward to accept Christ at a Billy Graham Crusade as well as at the Salvation Army, but nothing had happened, nothing had changed. She told me that I didn't believe. I started arguing with her, but she insisted. Finally she told me that I had to believe 100%. As she continued to talk, I felt something stirring in my heart. I knew that I had never really believed.

Once I understood that I had to believe it all in order to be a Christian, it made sense, it made a difference. I walked out of her office and got down on my knees and asked God to come into my life - this time fully understanding what I was doing.

When I asked God to forgive me of my sins, I clearly heard Him say to me, "I can forgive you of your sins, but why can't you forgive yourself?" I knew at that point that I had just met God.

I did not sleep for four days. My life had changed. I started reading the Bible every day. My recovery began.

A Christian guard at the prison befriended me. He was a great influence on me and not only helped me with my Christian faith, but also did a lot to protect me. We became prayer buddies. I began to see just how God was working in my life through this prison experience even though it was never easy.

As I neared the end of my sentence, I called my father. It was the first conversation we had had in years. I told him about the Lord and what God was doing in my life, and I discovered that my dad was reading the Bible as well.

God had come to me while I was in prison. When I was released, I knew I was a changed man. I got involved in a Bible-teaching church and invited my parents who, in time, gave their hearts to the Lord. Today I am married with two children, and I am serving God by leading prayer meetings in the local jail. Just as God came to me in prison and began to heal me of my addictions and emotional scars, I am now trying to bring that same hope to others who are at the end of their rope.

"I was naked and you clothed Me; I was sick and you visited Me;
I was in prison and you came to Me."
Matthew 25:36

THINK ABOUT THIS

Anger, frustration, abuse, self-hatred, dishonesty, and more all seem to be ingredients that exist in many of our lives at one time or another. Certainly some of us can identify with Grady's story. For others, we may shake our heads and wonder if it can all be true - one life so horribly riddled with trauma. It seems that Grady didn't have a fair chance at life from childhood on.

How many times have we come across a situation, perhaps even in our own lives, when we felt helpless because our needs were so great? There was nothing that Grady could do, even though he had found religion, been counseled by the best, and even experienced a season of reprieve. The haunting grip of destruction still held him.

So what changed? Grady's perspective changed. He came to a place of finally surrendering control and fully believing what he had heard countless times. The message of the cross, forgiveness, the resurrection, and restoration are all true. God is in the business of restoring broken lives and loves us more than we can imagine.

QUESTIONS WE SHOULD ASK

How has anger infiltrated your life without you even realizing it?

Do you live with unnecessary guilt that you would like to get rid of?

If you were to conduct an analysis of your life, are you in need of healing in one area or another?

Appendix . . .

Anger, Guilt, Healing

eighteen

C H L O E   F A I T H ' S   S T O R Y

A Daisy that Bloomed in a Storm

"Then, as we stared at the picture of the second sonogram,
we wept. Our baby had a normal body and a normal face,
but, at closer examination, the horrific truth was uncovered
- our baby didn't have a brain or the top of her skull."

I was elated when I found out I was pregnant. Albert and I had a three-year-old child and were ready to add on to our family. Everywhere we turned there seemed to be a sign telling us it was time to conceive. We even won a drawing from our church raffle - a romantic night for two at a plush hotel in the city.

I conceived, but my dream-come-true soon turned into a nightmare. A routine test three months into my pregnancy indicated that something might be wrong with my unborn baby. A Level-Two sonogram would determine specifically what was wrong, if anything. There was always that possibility that the first test results were wrong.

The wait seemed endless. For ten days my husband and I prayed that everything would be all right. Then, as we stared at the picture of the second sonogram, we wept. Our baby had a normal body and a normal face, but, at closer examination, the horrific truth was uncovered - our baby didn't have a brain or the top of her skull. There was nothing above the eyebrows. There was only a brain stem, and it was that brain stem that was keeping her alive.

The medical team encouraged me to abort, but Albert and I refused. We stood alone in our convictions. Even our families wanted us to consider abortion. Everyone assumed that we were bringing heartache on ourselves by keeping the baby. People even ridiculed us. It was a very tough time.

The baby continued to grow in my womb. As time went on, I started feeling her kick, and with each kick I thanked the Lord she was still alive. Although the doctors predicted I would miscarry, I believed that the baby would make it to full term.

The baby's heart was incredibly strong. I continued to go to my doctor's appointments like normal, and eventually he and the nurse were supportive of our stand to continue the pregnancy.

Albert and I knew there was a reason for this trial. A few years earlier, we had come to know God and His love. The circumstances we faced with this difficult pregnancy only led us to a deeper sense of His loving care. We felt Him beside us every step of the way. There were times when I would cry or be paralyzed with fear, but God gave me the strength to endure. If I had not been able to pray to Him, I would have definitely lost it. I knew He had a purpose for all of this, and most of the time I rested in that knowledge.

God encouraged us in curious ways. For example, our three-year-old son loved Moses. He would often speak about the burning bush and the different ways that God spoke to his hero. Albert and I were amused by our son's interest in Moses, but what we didn't know was that God would use his fascination to make Himself real to us.

One day, while setting up our new computer, I decided to download a particular program. The temporary password was "emptyscalp719." I immediately got frightened. In fact, I was so spooked by it that I refused to turn on the computer for days. I could not get that password out of my mind.

Another day, while my husband and I were driving in the car, I happened to look up in the sky. "Look," I said. Chiseled in the cloud was a formation that looked like a picture of Moses with his hand outstretched holding a baby. My husband pulled the car over and got out to look. He saw it too. We were astonished, and we knew right then and there that God was with us. He was lifting us up and giving us hope. We began reading the book of Deuteronomy in the Bible, where so much of what we know about Moses is written. I thought about the computer program and the eerie temporary password, "emptyscalp719."

I just couldn't get that password out of my mind. It seemed odd, but the Lord led us to Deuteronomy 7:19 to see what it says. I was amazed when I read the verse: "...the great trials which your eyes saw, the signs and the wonders, the mighty hand and the outstretched arm, by which the Lord your God brought you out." Everything came together in that one verse. The great trial our eyes saw was the picture of our baby on the sonogram. The signs and wonders were all of these little indicators, including the computer password, that God was with us. The outstretched arm was the sign we saw in the clouds. There was no doubt in our minds that God was with us, cared about us, and would use our baby for His glory.

My doctor started talking about organ donation. Though we had never thought of that before, Albert and I got excited at the thought that our baby could help another child live. We began to think that maybe this was the purpose the Lord had in mind for our unborn child. We met with the donor procurement team. After a few tests and blood work, everything was in order to donate our baby's organs at birth. In fact, within a short time, a need came in for a liver transplant for an infant residing in another state.

We named the baby Chloe (which means "blooming") Faith. Her name described what my husband and I experienced throughout the entire pregnancy. This little baby's life was the catalyst for our own blooming faith in God.

Even though Chloe Faith had been in a normal position and I was scheduled for a routine delivery, she soon turned around in the womb and was breach. If she was delivered breach, there was a high likelihood that she would suffocate, which would render her organs useless. The doctor scheduled a Cesarean delivery for me.

Chloe Faith was born at 7:55 a.m. With the procurement team waiting, there was a fifteen-minute window during which the organs could be transferred and still be healthy and vital. But little Chloe kept breathing and crying. One of the nurses swaddled her in a blanket and brought her over to me. I kissed her a few times on the cheek. The team waited, checking her vitals. Chloe kept breathing.

Everyone waited. Too much time passed, and the organ transplant had to be called off. During that time my husband and I actually prayed the Lord would take her home in order that the other child might be saved. That was the only time that we cried out to God and asked Him, "Why?" We thought the reason for Chloe's life was to save another child, but now that purpose was removed.

Actually, God had the perfect plan for Chloe's life. As each family member and friend came and saw her, Albert and I watched many hard hearts being instantly softened. The room was filled that day with loved ones who just wanted to hold and kiss little Chloe. The very same baby that so many thought should have been aborted was now leaving her touch forever on all their lives.

Chloe Faith lived twenty-two hours. Everyone, including the medical team, cried when she took her last breath.

Today, I am pregnant with our third child. Chloe Faith lives on, not only in heaven with God, but in the hearts of her family and the medical team that played a part in her brief but blessed day here on earth.

"My brethren, count it all joy when you fall into various trials, knowing that the testing of your faith produces patience. But let patience have its perfect work, that you may be perfect and complete, lacking nothing."
James 1:2-4

THINK ABOUT THIS

Just when you think you've got life's plan all figured out, God shows you a better one. God's plan for little Chloe Faith was to live and bless the lives of those who loved her. It was that simple. Her life was cherished in God's eyes. With our human minds, it would seem that to save another infant's life would have been a better plan, but for God, Chloe's life was valuable just because He loved her.

When you consider your own life, you may wonder if it means very much to God. Some of us feel as though we really don't count here on earth, or perhaps that God hasn't used us a whole lot in the big scheme of things. Then, when you read a story like this one, you realize how precious each of us is to God. Then you begin to understand that we are here just to love and be loved by God.

The Bible tells us that God counts the hairs on our head (Matthew 10:30). That's a God who truly loves His children! Take time today and meditate on God's love for you. It's deeper than the deepest ocean and higher than the highest mountain. He really loves you.

QUESTIONS WE SHOULD ASK

Think of three ways God has shown you His love this week.

Do you value the life of the unborn? Is this something you need to rethink?

Are you looking for guidance in a difficult situation? List several ways God might have been speaking to you about this.

Appendix . . .

Love of God, Abortion, Guidance

nineteen

C H E T ' S   S T O R Y

In the Face of Danger

"I prayed that God would take the wind away, but He didn't.
Then I prayed that He would calm the sea, but He didn't.
Finally I prayed that the rain would stop, but it didn't.
I remember thinking, 'Lord, if I die, this won't
make You look good. Don't You know that I am on my
way to rescue my wife?'"

I grew up in a strong Christian home. My desire to be a missionary was birthed in my youth. At the age of thirteen, when most boys are enjoying their friends and starting to think about girls, I was on my way to Liberia for my second mission trip of the summer.

That trip impacted my life. I immediately bonded with the Liberian people. I was able to relate to them, and they with me. At age thirteen, God planted the seed for my future calling.

I was in my last semester at Florida Atlantic University when I met Andrea, and we became close friends. I considered medical school, but I felt more drawn to go to Liberia to teach for a year. That seed, which God had sown in my youth, had already taken root.

Andrea and I corresponded the whole time I was in Liberia. We fell in love across the miles. When I returned to the United States in 1992, I proposed to her, and we were married in March of 1994. She had prayed for a godly man who had a heart for missions, and she felt I was definitely that man. In marrying me, however, she knew she was also committing herself to a life in Liberia. When our first child was five months old, we packed up and moved there.

Liberia is a country largely influenced by American culture. It was founded on the ideals of freedom and democracy. In fact, American law students wrote the Liberian constitution.

In 1989, civil unrest took hold and threatened the country's freedom. Revolutionaries plotted to overthrow the government. During the 1990s, the country had no organized leadership. Civil war began to ravage the nation, making Liberia a dangerous environment, especially for Americans.

For our first two months in Liberia, Andrea and the baby and I stayed in the capital city of Monrovia before settling three hours inland in Buchanan. I had a burden on my heart to minister to the Bassa people who were living in refugee camps. They needed a school as well as relief aid for other war-related problems, such as hunger, sickness, and disease. There was basically nothing left of their society.

Our job was sometimes overwhelming, but we learned to rely on God. We didn't realize that the obstacles we faced daily were actually a training ground for the more serious trouble that was ahead.

The war left many orphans in Liberia. I always wanted a big family, so when a woman who lived in our community died in childbirth and left her two-year-old son without a family, Andrea and I decided to adopt him. This was the beginning of us extending our family beyond racial lines.

The unrest in Liberia escalated into the streets and villages. Fear was rampant among the people, and fighting occurred every day.

One day a group of soldiers began menacingly waving their rifles and automatic weapons in the streets of our town, resulting in an outbreak of rebellion. I quickly moved Andrea and our two boys back to Monrovia to be near the U.S. Embassy in case there was a need for evacuation. Then I went on to Ghana to work with the United Nations to help retrieve food for the people. While I was in Ghana, I learned that Liberia had broken out in a full-scale war.

There was no communication in or out of the country. At first I thought it might not be as serious as it sounded since skirmishes and violence had become an everyday occurrence. I called my parents to see if they had spoken to Andrea. The last conversation they had with her was the week before. While they were talking to her, they could hear the sounds of gunfire in the background. They hadn't heard anything since.

The next day, my team and I went to the airport to fly back to Liberia. I thought, "Once we are all together, we can go through anything." But my hope was gone when we found out that the airport in Monrovia had been burned and destroyed. "Burned? What do you mean, burned?" I refused to accept this headline. The very city that I moved my family to for their safety was now besieged by war!

My only mission was to save my wife and children - and soon! But there was another problem. I was holding an expired visa for the Ivory Coast, and I had to get across that border in order to get back into Liberia. If the border patrol checked me, I would be detained and have to wait weeks before I could get a new visa.

The next morning I boarded a bus for the border, which was about eight hours away, with 100 nationals. At our first checkpoint, the immigration police stopped the bus to check everyone's passports. This was it! I was done for! One by one, the officer checked our papers. One passenger was sent off the bus, then another, and another. I was sitting in the last row and began praying desperately to the Lord for His mercy. Finally my turn came. I was so nervous that my hand shook as I opened my backpack. I prayed frantically, yet the police officer still hovered over me with his hand extended waiting for me to give him my papers. "What am I going to do? Doesn't the Lord know I need to get to my wife?" I thought. "Oh, God, please help me!" I whispered. I pulled out my expired visa, and just then the officer hit me on shoulder and gestured for me to return my documents to my bag! My body went limp. My blood didn't know if it should curdle or thin. The Lord had parted the sea and paved the way!

That night my friend and I arrived at the border town. The only way we could get into Liberia now was by canoe. We chartered a crew, got into the thirty-foot vessel, and began the grueling four-day trip to Liberia. For twenty-four hours we wrestled against the rough ocean along the West Africa coast. That first night the crew ate all the food.

As we pulled up to the water's edge on the last evening, rebel soldiers were waiting for us. I felt as if a million eyes were watching me from every angle. My friend and I hung back as our crew captain spoke to one of the leaders who held a big gun in his hand. The leader walked confidently toward me and said, "So, you are the man who pulls bullets out of the people we put them in," and then he walked away. Shortly thereafter, a woman came up to us and told us to hide because she had overheard the rebels talking about how they were going to kill us. We found an abandoned building and hid there. But in the middle of the night, we woke up sensing we had to leave. We found our crew and talked them into going back out onto the ocean.

As we started rowing into the calm, dark waters, we noticed headlights offshore. I looked at the large boat stationed in the port and saw another canoe moving behind it. It was coming after us! We kept rowing, and then, all of a sudden, the dead calm waters turned into a raging sea. Monsoon winds came out of nowhere. I prayed that God would take the wind away, but He didn't. Then I prayed that He would calm the sea, but He didn't. Finally I prayed that the rain would stop, but it didn't. I remember thinking, "Lord, if I die, this won't make You look good. Don't You know that I am on my way to rescue my wife?" We were all getting sick and having a difficult time trying to stay afloat. For three hours the storm beat down on us before it finally subsided. The crew hated me for forcing them onto the sea. Throughout the storm they hurled insults at me. I retreated deep into the hull of the canoe. I was angry and confused and felt deserted in my greatest hour of need. I couldn't understand why God hadn't answered my prayers.

We finally arrived on land sun-beaten, dehydrated, hungry, and tired. Friends there fed us and nursed our wounds. The next day we went back to port to board a boat heading for Monrovia where Andrea was supposedly staying. The same woman, who a couple of nights before had warned us to hide from the rebels, was there at the port. She approached me, shouting, "You are blessed, you are blessed, you are blessed!" Then she said that the night we escaped, the canoe that had been following us was filled with rebel soldiers armed with machine guns. The rebels chased us all the way to the river's mouth, but the fierce storm that came out of nowhere forced them back! I was completely humbled! My worst nightmare on that open sea was actually my greatest blessing. My lament about unanswered prayer had become a testimony of God's grace. It was the monsoon that God used to save our lives!

While I was fighting my way back to Andrea, she was battling her own horror. Missionaries were being evacuated, but she couldn't leave because she had our birth child and our adopted Liberian child, and the adoption papers were burning in the city of Monrovia. She kept telling the Liberian officials that they were both her children, but because one was black, they had a hard time believing her. She had no choice but to stay where she was with the children.

One day the rebels came to the apartment where Andrea, the

children, and others were staying. They stared right at her as they took one of the babies and threw him around like a rag doll. After pointing a gun and threatening all the missionaries, they said that they would come back later that evening to rape Andrea; then they left. The Liberians Andrea was staying with told her that if she stayed, they would all be dead. So the next morning she determined to try and make her way to a missionary compound across the street. This was no small task. She had two infant children, she was white and stood out like a sore thumb, and the rebels were running wild shooting anything that moved. The scene was sickening. People were stabbing each other. Dead bodies were strewn about the roads and walkways. The carnage was disgusting. The rebels were using the inner parts of dead human beings as checkpoints along the street.

When I finally arrived in Monrovia, a car was waiting and drove us into town. I ran to the military base and made a huge scene begging them to take me to my wife. I broke down, turned, and walked out the door and into the street. A van filled with Russian pilots en route to the American Embassy stopped. They picked me up, and I went with them to the American Embassy. People who were trying to get out of the country stormed the Embassy. Just as our van pulled up to the gates, a truck filled with rebels pulled alongside and started to fire. The Embassy gate suddenly opened, and we drove onto American grounds and into safety.

The Embassy staff was shocked to see me alive. My mother had just talked to them an hour before. She told them I was on my way to Monrovia, but they said that it would be impossible for me to make it. Imagine the looks on their faces when I walked in! There was no doubt that God had protected me and brought me back to my family.

Then I found out the Marines had evacuated my wife and kids to the Ivory Coast.

When I called my mom to tell her I was okay, she said she had been praying for Andrea and the kids' safety when she turned on CNN and actually saw Andrea and the children getting into a Marine helicopter in the background! God had shown her, literally, that they were safe.

That same day I was evacuated and reunited with my family.

Andrea and I have lived through a trial by fire and a true test of our faith. Both of us have faced insurmountable odds and frightening experiences. We were scared and at times even thought God had forgotten about us. Yet, in the midst of all this, we came to know the Lord in a much deeper way. We discovered that He is real, He cares about us, and He will go to any length to protect us. When our prayers appeared to go unanswered, it was because He was answering them in a far greater way.

Today we live in Florida. We adopted two other Liberian children and had two more of our own. Our hearts will always be with the Liberian people, and we are waiting on the Lord to show us if He will use us again in that country in the future.

> "God is our refuge and strength,
> A very present help in trouble."
> Psalm 46:1

THINK ABOUT THIS

Have you ever felt as though you've been forgotten? We've all experienced it in one way or another. We face a trial or trauma and wonder if God even hears our prayers and cries for help. We plead with Him and ask why He would possibly allow something so awful to happen to us.

Sometimes, like Chet, we see God's protection at the end of our suffering. More often, though, we never know the exact reason for our pain. God tells us that He will bring good out of every situation, not that every situation will be good. We need to come to a place of trusting God and believing that someday we will understand.

The Bible says, "For our light and momentary troubles are achieving for us an eternal glory that far outweighs them all"(2 Corinthians 4:17). Someday, from heaven, our troubles on earth will look light and momentary compared to all God has waiting for us in heaven. The question is whether or not we will look back at our time here and be able to say that we honored God regardless of what we had to go through.

QUESTIONS WE SHOULD ASK

Can you think of a situation in your life that you need perseverance in order to get through?

Do you need to walk across a perilous road, but fear is keeping you from doing so?

List two areas in your life where you need God's protection. Pray for it.

Appendix . . .

Perseverance, Fear, Protection

twenty

A M A N D A ' S   S T O R Y

A Bicycle Built for Two

"My heart's desire was for a shiny, perfect, purple bicycle, but God had it in His heart to use that longing to give me much, much more..."

I had walked past that storefront window countless times. There it was - a shiny, purple, and perfect new bicycle.

There are just some things that all children want, and I was no exception. "Oh, the things I could do with that beautiful new bike!" I thought.

My father was a pastor, and our family did not have a lot of money, so I decided to save my allowance and odd-job money to buy myself the bicycle. Every week I walked past the store to see "my" beautiful purple bike.

I worked hard to save my money and kept praying that God would bring me what I wanted.

One day during Sunday school, my teacher talked about a missionary family in need. She told us about the horrible sickness this family was enduring. Reading from a letter written by the family, she told the class about the little boy who had contracted hepatitis, most likely from a typhoid shot he had received in Chile. All week I thought about that little boy far away in Chile.

The next Sunday my teacher asked us what we should do to help this little boy. All the children decided he could really use a brand new bike - that would cheer him up for sure! I remember my heart almost stopping. I said, "Oh no, God, not my bike!" But then I knew I had to give my bike money to my teacher so it could help that little boy in Chile get a bike.

One week later, I gave my money to the teacher.

Many years later in college, I began praying that God would send me a godly husband.

My father was still a pastor and was also teaching at a local Baptist college. When I went home for Christmas vacation one year, I met Philip at my father's church. Philip was attending the Baptist college where my father taught. In fact, he was in his class.

Not long after my Christmas break, I decided to transfer to this same college. I got to know Philip better since my college roommate was engaged to his best friend and my parents and Philip's parents were also friends.

Our first date was on Valentine's Day. It soon became obvious that we were made for each other. We decided to get married. I didn't know then just how God-ordained our relationship was.

One evening, after both our families had eaten dinner together, Philip's mom started reminiscing about their missionary days and what life was like on the field with small children. She shared about a time in Chile when the whole family had been terribly sick and how Philip had come down with hepatitis, presumably from a typhoid shot. I couldn't believe what I was hearing! My husband was the little boy that I had given up my bike money for! He was the very one that God had put on my heart to help! I had to leave the room because I was so emotional - I just could not stop crying.

God had been so good to me. My heart's desire was for a shiny, perfect, purple bicycle, but God had it in His heart to use that longing to give me much, much more - a godly husband that He had ordained from the very beginning.

Philip and I now have three grown children and have been married for twenty-nine years. We know in our hearts and hold onto the fact that God made us for each other and planned it that way before even time began.

> *"And everyone who has left houses or brothers or sisters or father or mother or wife or children or lands, for My name's sake, shall receive a hundredfold."*
> *Matthew 19:29*

THINK ABOUT THIS

Obedience is never an easy thing. We struggle with it from the time we are born. And, yet, it's through obedience that we learn and grow as individuals. If we disobey our parents, we're punished; if we disobey our boss, we get fired. We all have to obey someone.

God wants to bless us spiritually, physically, and emotionally. More importantly, He wants us to learn to obey His promptings as Amanda did so that we can become all He created us to be.

The Bible says, "Obey me, and I will be your God and you will be my people. Walk in all the ways I command you, that it may go well with you" (Jeremiah 7:23).

QUESTIONS WE SHOULD ASK

Do you get impatient waiting for things to happen in your life and try to make them happen on your own?

Are you able to hear God's whispers through your conscience? How do you respond when you hear them?

List three blessings you have received by being obedient to God in a particular area of your life.

Appendix . . .

Obedience, Prayer, Providence of God

DOUG AND CATHERINE'S STORY

Looking for Love

> *"We were living together, we were not married, and yet no one from the church said a word to us. That was just the way it was. Looking back now, that seems odd."*

Paths have a way of winding in and out of trees and other scenic landscapes. These same paths, however, can often trail through rocky terrain and dangerous brush. What starts out appearing beautiful soon becomes ugly and treacherous.

In the same way, as we walk down the path of life, we often partake in those situations that initially are pleasant and fun, only to find out farther down the road that the very things that seemed so appealing were in reality destructive.

Doug and Catherine know of such paths.

Later in their lives, their paths would meet, and though there would be wonderful fun and much joy, there would also be enormous heartache.

D O U G ' S S T O R Y

Life was pretty normal for me, at least as a child. Born and raised in the Midwest Bible Belt, I grew up going to church and doing all the typical things that a small town boy would do, but I struggled with feelings of insecurity.

I was shorter, thinner, and weighed much less than the other boys in school. Although I gave it every effort, it was difficult for me to compete in sports. I hung around with two groups of kids who called themselves Christians. However, while some of these kids really lived out their faith, many of them were Christians in name only.

My family moved to Florida in my senior year of high school. I wanted to join the Navy after I graduated, but my parents insisted that I go to college, so I enrolled in the University of Florida and majored in history and religion.

Still feeling less than and hoping to be accepted, I quickly got into the fraternity scene. I found myself in a new world of parties where drinking ruled. It was a time of change in America. Innocence was lost, and young people were looking for meaning in the midst of the Viet Nam War. Constraints and values were thrown over, and many of us, who thought we were living free, were actually becoming enslaved to the very currencies of our so-called "freedom."

Alcohol allowed me to do the things I couldn't do for myself, like open up and become the life of the party. I was pretty shy by nature and inhibited, but when I drank, I was the guy that people wanted to be around. I was charming to the girls, and that opened up a whole other world for me.

I didn't know at the time that this seemingly good antidote to my shyness would change into a devastating noose around my neck. My social drinking frequently ended in episodes of blackouts. My grades dropped, and I lost all interest in studies. My life existed of parties, sex, and alcohol. I felt no motivation to do anything with my life except just have fun. Eventually, the draft board caught up with me, and I registered with the Naval Reserve.

The Navy stationed me in Key West. Although I began to learn new things and meet new friends, I felt very alone. Many times I would pass by the chaplain's office and wonder about God. I never stopped to talk to him. Instead, I spent my time chasing women, alcohol, and parties.

After I got out of the Navy, I met a girl and proposed to her within a week, and within three months, we were married. I got a job in the boating industry and tried to limit my drinking to weekends only. Occasionally I blacked out, but for the most part, I was a fairly functional alcoholic. I was a responsible father, and I never missed a day of work or got a D.U.I. or had any of the other signposts, all of which kept me in denial about my drinking problem. Eventually, I started drinking every night.

When my brother began going to Alcoholics Anonymous, I saw changes in him that I liked and even envied. He encouraged me to go with him, and finally I did. It was a relief for me to hear people talk about the real things of life. I heard my story repeated again and again among the many people that were in the room. I was only 34 years old at the time, but because of the alcohol, I was tired all the time. I managed to stay sober in AA, but my marriage started to fall apart, and soon my wife and I were divorced.

I felt the marriage was beyond repair, so I just forged ahead on my own. I had custody of my son, and I began having relationships with other women. I switched addictions, basically. And, I was still lonely. I know now that I was seeking a fulfillment that only God can give.

C A T H E R I N E ' S   S T O R Y

At seven years old, my family moved from New York to Florida. It was a traumatic upheaval for me. During my growing-up years in Florida, my dad took us to church on a regular basis, although my mother would only accompany us at Christmas and Easter. These Sundays at church became a cornerstone of fond memories. I knew about God, I prayed to Him every night, and I knew that He loved me. I continued going to church throughout my teens, but I also got caught up in my looks. I found that getting attention from guys made me feel good about myself. Gaining their interest gave me a sense of worth and a feeling of beauty. It was the beginning of a pattern of preservation that worked for many years.

After high school, I started to date. I met my husband-to-be a year after graduation. I was nineteen years old. We bought a house and planned the wedding. Although I had strong reservations, I didn't want to hurt anyone. The invitations had been sent and the dress bought, so I went through with the wedding. After three months of marriage, I started to despair. I finally confided in my mother-in-law who told me, "Catherine, you've made your bed, now lie in it." I went to my mother and shared my feelings with her, and she told me that I would learn to love him. After three months, I walked out. However, I went to counseling and eventually went back to my husband and stayed with him for eleven years.

In the course of my eleven-year marriage, I was mostly miserable. I left four or five times, spending the weekend with my sister, searching my soul about my marriage and contemplating what to do. I always ended up going back, thinking it would be different, but nothing changed. My self-image and sense of value came entirely from men. I continually wanted their attention. If a man was attracted to me or flirted with me, it made me feel worthwhile, special, and pretty. I had a bottomless pit in me - a void that, really, no man could fill.

When our first child was two years old, we decided to go to church. One day, while I was working as a committee member for the church boat parade, I met Doug.

O U R   S T O R Y

Doug was divorced, but I was still married when we first spoke to each other over the phone. We both had children enrolled in the same church school, and we both considered ourselves Christians. In fact, if anyone were to ask Doug or me if we were Christians, we both would have said, "Absolutely." We knew all about God, or at least thought that we did, but, although I knew about Him, I really didn't know Him, and Doug's relationship with Him was based on his crying out to Him in emergencies. He had, so to speak, a 911-GOD.

We were very attracted to each other. We met discreetly, at various locations and times. Eight months after we met, I filed for divorce. Two weeks after the divorce was final, I moved in with him. There we were - Doug and his son, my two children, and me - all living together in this tiny house.

In our new life together, we all attended church on a regular basis. It's really amazing that no one said anything to us. We were living together, we weren't married, and yet no one from the church said a word to us. That was just the way it was. Looking back now, that seems odd.

We both started to think about marriage - just not at the same time! When I talked about marriage, Doug wasn't ready. When Doug talked about marriage, I didn't feel ready. Finally, after a year and a half, we got married.

Doug thought that I was absolutely everything he wanted in a woman. I felt the same way about him. We were both so enamored with each other that I would say we really became each other's god.

Life was good. Money was no problem, so we moved into a much nicer home, and I stopped working. We went skiing, we traveled to Europe, and Doug even took flying lessons.

In my previous marriage, I had attended a Christian retreat, and so

I encouraged Doug to go. After much deliberation, he decided to attend. It was a monumental turning point for him in his life and in his relationship with God. It was the first time ever that Doug knew he was important to God and that he couldn't dance around the issue of God's love any longer. God had been calling out to him all his life, and that call of love needed to be fortified by Bible study, prayer, and action for God's kingdom. During the weekend, Doug surrendered his life to God.

When I picked him up from the retreat, I asked him how it went. He could not respond, he only wept and told me that he truly met God that weekend for the first time and knew things were going to be all right.

We started attending prayer groups. We hosted Bible studies in our home and prayed and read the Bible together every morning. Our lives were moving forward with God. . . for a while.

About nine months later, Doug and I went to Switzerland on a ski trip. Shortly after our return home, I went to Colorado with some friends for another three-day ski trip. Doug gave me his blessing.

While I was at the lodge, I met a man, and there was an instant attraction. I ended up spending most of the three days around him, skiing, talking, eating, and walking. There was no doubt that my old patterns were resurfacing – the feelings of worth that would rise up when a man was attracted to me. I could feel myself getting pulled in, and I knew I was in trouble.

When I got home, Doug could tell something was wrong with me. I acted like a robot. My mind was always thinking about this man in Colorado. He consumed my thoughts. He asked repeatedly what was wrong, and I said, "Nothing," but he knew something was going on.

I started a phone relationship with him. He became my fix and my means of escape. When I talked to him on the phone, I felt okay for a while, but the next day I needed to talk to him again to feel up. I was living in an emotional whirlwind that was taking me down. Doug said that it was as if I were another woman, a woman he had never met. It was as if somebody had stolen my soul.

Doug insisted that we go to counseling. Though hesitant at first, I agreed to go if we could meet with a woman, since I felt a woman would understand my emotions far better than a man could.

One day Doug told the counselor, "Something's up – you'd better get her to tell me the truth because I am tired of living on the edge." It was then that I confessed that I had had an affair with the man in Colorado and promptly told Doug that I wanted to move to Colorado and be free.

However, I made a commitment to stay in counseling for three months before filing for divorce. Doug struggled with his feelings in those three months. He said he felt like God had kicked him in the teeth. He blamed God more than he blamed me. He said that he had finally come to know God, was walking in His ways, and yet his life was crumbling around him.

One day Doug's AA friend came to see him. Doug told him what he was planning to do to this guy in Colorado and how he was going to get even with me. His friend kept saying, "Doug, you have to do what's best for you." Doug kept on talking and his friend kept listening and repeating, "You have to do what's best for you." Finally Doug stopped venting and asked him, "What *is* best for me?" and his friend answered, "Forgive her."

This really impacted Doug, but I still wanted to leave.

It was a Friday night at the end of August, my reservations for Colorado were made for the following Tuesday. I sat on the porch, filled with despair and feeling like I was being pulled in two directions and about to have a nervous breakdown. I was shaking and sobbing, and I cried out to the Lord, "I can't do this anymore! I just can't do this anymore!"

Totally wracked and exhausted, I went to bed. Then, about two o'clock in the morning, I woke up with a start. I heard an actual, audible voice that said, "Don't go. Don't go." As incredible as that sounds, that's what happened.

I decided to stay, and Doug and I started seeing a Christian counselor this time. Doug also went to a men's accountability group. He worked on his own relationship with God, left me in God's hands, and stopped hovering over me.

It was a long road, and for six months into the counseling, Doug still felt numb. We both did, actually, yet we stayed in the marriage out of obedience to God.

The following February, I went to a healing service at a local church and heard an evangelist speak about healings of the heart. I went forward and asked the Lord, "God, heal me of whatever You want to heal me of because there is so much!" I had finally surrendered.

In the next few months, I slowly began to feel that my self-worth was coming from God, not men. I began to experience God filling the void that men could never fill. My friends even noticed a peacefulness in me.

Three years later, Doug and I started to attend a new church that taught chapter by chapter, verse by verse from the Bible. Today we know that God used this church to help heal our marriage.

"Life will never be perfect," says Doug. "But, it can be good - and it can be joyful - no matter what the circumstances. Following God made all the difference in our lives."

*"Trust in the Lord with all your heart,
and lean not on your own understanding;
in all your ways acknowledge Him, and
He shall direct your paths."*
Proverbs 3:5,6

"I can do all things through Christ who strengthens me."
Philippians 4:13

THINK ABOUT THIS

We tend to think that when we get married, love will carry us through. We're taught to believe that it happens naturally for two people to get married and live happily ever after. After all, it happened that way for Cinderella, right?

Soon after the wedding, however, we realize that marriage is a lot of work, and the one you married will never be the perfect spouse you dreamed of. We believed our partner would fill the void in our heart and complete us, and we get frustrated when he or she doesn't.

The real problem is that the void we're trying to fill is a void only God can satisfy. He is the One who can complete us. As we allow God to fill our hearts, we have more to give to the one we love. If you are struggling with your relationship, go to God first, then watch what He'll do in your marriage.

QUESTIONS WE SHOULD ASK

Are you trying to take away the emptiness in your life through a relationship?

Doug escaped from his feelings of insecurity through alcohol. How do you escape from your problems and feelings?

Just as Jesus makes forgiveness available to us, we need to be quick to forgive others. Is there anyone in your life right now that you need to forgive?

Appendix . . .

Insecurity, Alcohol Abuse, Forgiveness

J O S H U A ' S   S T O R Y

When Life Changes in a Moment

> *"My son was lying motionless; he was purple and foaming at the mouth. The dog was barking hysterically, and everything was happening so quickly."*

It is a moment every mother and father are sure can only happen to someone else, a moment we all pray will never happen to us.

My husband, Marcus, and I were from the modern "peace, love, and granola" culture, adjusting to a yuppie world, so to speak. Avid water sports fans, we loved swimming, scuba diving, and boating. We made the water a significant part of our lives. Even our relationship began as a shipboard romance. Marcus was working as a boat captain on a luxury yacht where I was the chef.

We soon married and came ashore. I was a stay-at-home wife while Marcus continued with his career in yacht management. Our lives were all about the water, so naturally one of our prerequisites in finding a home was that it had to have a swimming pool.

Our son, Joshua, was born at home and grew up in and around the water. As soon as he was able to walk, we signed him up for survival swimming classes!

One day, tragedy struck, and our lives changed in a moment.

It was a bright, sunny Thursday morning, and I was busy getting ready for a weekend scuba diving trip. Marcus and I had been looking forward to the trip for quite some time. Joshua was riding his tricycle around the perimeter of the pool, almost within arm's reach, while I was making some phone calls. The sliding glass doors were all open to the soft, tropical breezes, and although my back was to the pool, I could hear Joshua "Fred-Flintstoning" around the patio on his trike. After a few minutes, I suddenly realized that everything was quiet.... too quiet.

I quickly turned around. To my horror, Joshua was floating on top of the water face down with his little trike bobbing up and down close by. I screamed and dropped the phone. I ran to the edge of the pool. I screamed again. My neighbor heard me and rushed over, jumping the fence. We pulled Joshua out of the pool and immediately started to administer CPR. We called the police, and then I ran to call Marcus. It was 11:00 am.

I was frantic. My son was lying motionless; he was purple and foaming at the mouth. The dog was barking hysterically, and everything was happening so quickly. I kept telling Joshua to please come back to Mommy.

The fire department and paramedics arrived at the house and immediately began trying to resuscitate Joshua.

By the time Marcus got home, Joshua's small, pale, lifeless body was being wheeled out on a gurney to the awaiting ambulance. "I am so sorry," I cried as I climbed into the ambulance with my son. Totally distraught, Marcus followed in his car, the image of his pale, too-still child strapped onto the gurney haunting his mind.

A special pediatric trauma team was waiting for us in the emergency room. They whisked Joshua down the hall behind large doors. We allowed the hospital staff to escort us into a special area where they asked us if we had a church. Joshua had probably been without oxygen or a heartbeat for more than twenty-five to 30 minutes by this time. It seemed a foregone conclusion that he would not make it.

But God had other plans.

Each time his heart started and stopped brought renewed hope followed by disappointment. Finally, his heart started beating on a regular basis. But Joshua had been without oxygen for too long, and the neurologists who examined him told us if he did survive, he would probably be brain dead. The first 72 hours would determine his fate.

Although we attended church, we were what Marcus calls closet Christians. From one moment in life to the next, we had found ourselves in total despair having to rely on God and not ourselves. We were soaked with fear and confusion, and in our desperate state, we turned to the Lord for answers.

Joshua was transferred to the pediatric intensive care unit. Then the waiting began.

Sitting there, hour after hour, I had plenty of time to think. Although Marcus never blamed me or pointed his finger at me, I felt tremendous guilt. I blamed myself over and over again. I kept thinking, "If only..." There were days when the feelings of sorrow and shame would swallow me. It was so hard to look at my son - to watch his suffering - and not feel that I was responsible for all of it. Hot and cold emotions and the tears and fears became almost unbearable.

Marcus and I held onto each other, determined not to allow this to drive a wedge between us. We knew that the death of a child often tears couples apart.

Somehow Joshua made it past the 72-hour danger period; however, most of the hospital staff did not have much hope that he would ever respond. But I was unwavering. I knew that my son would not only pull through, but he would once again smile at his mommy and daddy. I just could not accept that Joshua would remain in a vegetative state all the rest of his life.

Joshua was in so much pain that, at times, Marcus would retreat to the corner of the room and just cry. He wanted to trade places with his son. He longed to take Joshua's suffering away.

Friends, family, and church members gathered continually at the hospital to pray and give us encouragement. Day after day we waited. The neurologist was evasive about Joshua's condition, but Marcus finally insisted that he give us a prognosis. On a scale from 1-10, brain dead being a 10, the doctor put Joshua at an 8.

We still wouldn't give up. I would tell Joshua to fight and not listen to the doctors. I would be persistent in telling him to call on Jesus to help him. The doctors said Joshua could not hear, but I knew differently. We sought God's strength to help us deal with our son's accident, and our fears. We feared for the future - not knowing what each day would bring, and we feared for Joshua. What kind of life would he live? Would he ever be normal? Would he always be in pain? The questions seemed endless.

After 30 days Joshua was transferred out of intensive care and into a rehabilitation facility.

Due to the lack of oxygen, his brain had swelled, causing his body to twist in posture. He also lost five of his bottom front teeth from clenching his jaw and his inability to swallow. There was very little sign of cognitive life in him.

One of the doctors told Marcus that our lives had changed forever. Although we knew it was true, the thought made us angry. It was very hard to hear the truth. We would have given anything to change things back to the way they were before the accident. Yet, even in these seemingly impossible circumstances, God continued to work out His good purpose.

God gave us the strength to believe Joshua's life was not over. We started treating him just as we did before the accident, lavishing love and attention on him, talking to him, reading to him, and watching videos with him. We believed in our hearts that, behind his comatose state, Joshua was alive and well and able to feel and hear us.

Family, friends, and coworkers started a fund and bought us a special van. The expense of therapy, doctors' visits, and a wheelchair would be a challenge. Marcus eventually had to go back to work, while I spent my days at the rehab hospital caring for Joshua. Often the doctor's words would come back to me, and I would have to admit to myself that our life had certainly changed.

The staff told me Joshua couldn't see or hear, but I just didn't believe them. I would talk to Joshua, touch him, and treat him like I did before the accident. I needed to make life as normal as possible for him and for us. We had hope - something most of the hospital staff did not seem to possess.

Ever so slowly, Joshua started to respond. The true turning point came during a very simple moment.

I was putting Joshua's diaper on when I grabbed his little feet and said, "Pew, pew, Joshua's got stinky feet!" In that moment my son grinned and made a noise I wasn't sure of. Then I did it again. "Joshua has stinky little feet," I repeated. Again the same sound... Joshua had laughed! Marcus and I started crying and laughing at the same time. It was our first real sign that our son was coming back to us.

Two weeks later Joshua was released from the rehab hospital!

I took him to private therapy and started seeing miracle after miracle take place. Time and again, the doctors would predict that Joshua was not likely to respond or eat on his own or be able to think, and

Joshua would do just that! Eventually, he swallowed on his own and began responding to people around him. He could see, hear, and feel. He started to crawl and even began to communicate. God was working a miracle in our son's life. Every time the medical team said Joshua would never do something, he did it. It was evident that God's hand was on Joshua's life, although he was far from the normal child he once was.

Today Joshua is seven years old and in the 1st grade in public school. Unable to walk at this point, he spends his time in his wheelchair, but plays and learns just like the other children. In fact, Joshua does well in school.

It may very well be that he will never become your typical kid, but he is a very smart little boy, and he has accomplished the impossible, time and again. Marcus and I have learned that we cannot limit God. Our son's days are in His hands.

Yes, our lives have changed, but we are thankful now for this trial. Through it all, we met the living, loving God and discovered that He is more than sufficient for our every need.

"You made all the delicate, inner parts of my body and knit me together in my mother's womb. Thank You for making me so wonderfully complex! Your workmanship is marvelous — and how well I know it. You watched me as I was being formed in utter seclusion, as I was woven together in the dark of the womb. You saw me before I was born. Every day of my life was recorded in your book. Every moment was laid out before a single day had passed. How precious are your thoughts about me, O God! They are innumerable! I can't even count them; they outnumber the grains of sand! And when I wake up in the morning you are still with me!"
Psalm 139:13-18

THINK ABOUT THIS

Bad things do happen to good people, and good things do happen to bad people. No one really knows why or understands how. We come up with all kinds of theories and nice ideas, but the fact of the matter is we just don't know why little Joshua fell in the swimming pool that day. When we're lying in bed at night, if we're really honest with ourselves, we're just glad it didn't happen to us. We believe that if it had happened to us, we would never be able to handle it, but, if it does happen to you, you realize that you don't have a choice, and you deal with it.

The big question is how will you deal with it? Life isn't fair. The world is full of injustices. Sometimes little boys fall in swimming pools even when their moms and dads are listening for them while they play outside. There's no one to blame. It's just life. You can walk through your tragedy angry, bitter, and hating the world, or you can use your tragedy to help others who are suffering, to tell loved ones how much you love them, or to simply enjoy the good things life still has to offer.

The Bible says, "Even when the way goes through Death Valley, I'm not afraid when you walk at my side. Your trusty shepherd's crook makes me feel secure"(Psalm 23:4, The Message). Having God on our side during those dark nights will see us through.

QUESTIONS WE SHOULD ASK

Why do you think bad things happen to good people and good things happen to bad people?

What can we do when we face a tragedy and the anxiety is more than we can bear?

Do you know how to pray when you need God the most?

Appendix...

Providence of God, Anxiety, Prayer

twenty-four

J E F F ' S   S T O R Y

Without Explanation

*"By sixteen, I was skipping school. I looked like your
stereotypical drug addict. I had long hair and wore T-shirts
emblazoned with images of my favorite rock 'n roll band."*

I was a lonely boy. I had a family, but my two stepsisters were
considerably older than me, and I felt lonely and on my own. My
father died of cancer when I was a baby. Then I was molested at the
age of three by a family friend, and from then on I battled intense pent-
up anger and shame.

These emotions did not go away, so I sought any means possible to
escape from the inner torment they caused. One day, some of the older
kids in my neighborhood thought it would be fun to get this little kid
(me) stoned on marijuana to see what would happen. Their
"experiment" introduced me to an escape route that I would later take.

A few years passed, and something else happened that left me in even
greater turmoil. My stepsister had a son who was two years younger

than me. Craig was my buddy. We did everything together. Typical of young boys, we also argued. One day I let Craig ride my bike. He left it behind our family's pickup, and my sister ran over it when she backed the truck up. I was furious with him, and we started to argue. My sister tried to break up the fight. She loaded a lawn chair into the back of the pickup as we argued next over who would win the coveted position of riding on the chair in the back with the breeze blowing our hair rather than riding inside the stuffy old cab. After a few more minutes of this, I finally gave up and let Craig have the back of the truck.

As I climbed into the cab alongside my sister, I was so mad. I hated Craig at that moment and wished he were dead. I pouted as we rode down the street. Then, all of a sudden, there was a really loud noise. I turned to look out the back window, and I saw Craig and the lawn chair flying out of the truck! My sister stopped the truck and ran back to where Craig's body was lying in the middle of the road. I stood off in the distance staring, stunned. Craig didn't move. Soon the ambulance arrived. I knew my buddy was dead and was sure it was my fault.

That tragedy was the beginning of my escape into drugs. I was only eight years old and already wracked with confusion and despair. My only friend had been killed, and I felt responsible because I had wished him dead. I was convinced it was my fault. In fact, it took me more than a year after his funeral to actually cry for him. I just stuffed all my guilt and fear inside, which compacted my problems.

By the time I was eleven, I was getting high every day. It didn't take me long to figure out that the more I did drugs, the more popular I became with my friends.

Since we were smoking pot every day, my friends and I decided to start growing marijuana in a nearby orange grove. Soon we had our own supply of weed that we could smoke whenever we wanted. When we smoked we got destructive, throwing oranges at passing cars, vandalizing homes, and causing mischief wherever the opportunity presented itself.

As time went on, I became more and more violent. I would get into fights at school and even punch holes in the walls at home. Pot was not enough to drown my memories and feelings. I began to drink heavily and also started experimenting with harder drugs.

By sixteen, I was skipping school. I looked like your stereotypical drug addict. I had long hair and wore T-shirts emblazoned with images of my favorite rock 'n roll band. At the end of my ninth grade year, my mom enrolled me in a drug program.

I was in the program for ten months, and I did get clean. My friends who went to the same program were still getting high. I really believe now that God was the One who got me off the drugs, although at that point in my life, I wasn't somebody who prayed or even thought about God, for that matter.

I stopped the drugs, but I kept getting drunk on weekends. I was still a mess inside and trying to get away from the misery I felt. What I didn't know was that God was working for me behind the scenes.

After graduating from high school, I went home one day and found that a teacher's aide from my former school had dropped off a present for me. I opened it up and, seeing a Bible, thought, "This is a dumb gift." Needless to say, I tossed it in my room and didn't even open it.

I applied to a community college, and because I had not made good grades in high school, I had to do a lot of prep work just to get admitted. It took me about five and a half years to get my two-year degree, but I accomplished the task and managed an above average grade point average!

Near the end of my college courses, I started having chronic back problems. Sometimes the pain was so bad that I had to stand up in class. After a while, the pain began to shoot down my right leg. I went to a physical therapist who put me on an exercise program, but then the aching spread to my left leg as well. At times I was unable to walk because of the pain. I went to a doctor who ordered an MRI.

The MRI showed that I had a herniated disc in my back that was hitting against the sciatic nerve and causing the ache in my right leg, but that didn't explain the problem with my left leg. After further tests, they discovered I had a progressive bone cancer in my leg that, if left untreated, would lead to amputation.

The doctors wanted to remove the bone (all fourteen inches of it) and replace it with a donor bone. I began chemotherapy and spent more than 150 days in the hospital in a year's time. The thought of having a dead man's bone in my leg was a little nerve-wracking to me, but after my own bone broke three different times just from moving my leg, the operation sounded more appealing. When a donor bone was acquired, the doctors scheduled the operation.

The bone transplant was successful, but the chemotherapy took a toll on me. About six months into the treatments, a friend invited me to church. Feeling like I didn't have anything to lose, I decided to go.

I grew up in an agnostic home, so I was a bit skeptical. However, as soon as the pastor began to speak about God's love, I was intrigued and drawn to what he was saying.

I started to go to the church regularly. And at one particular service, I knew without a shadow of a doubt that God wanted to have a personal relationship with me. But it would be a couple of months more before I would experience His love in such a profound way that it would heal my inner agony.

I was progressively getting sicker from the cancer, but I was also experiencing more peace than I had ever known in my life.

One day when I was having a lot of pain in my leg and feeling very ill from the chemotherapy, I called my friend who had taken me to his church. He told me to read my Bible. When I hung up I looked around the living room for a Bible, but couldn't find one. Frustrated and sick, I got tears in my eyes and started to sit down. Just then, I remembered the Bible that I had gotten as a graduation present after high school. I tore my room apart until I found it. It was dusty because it had never been opened. Eight years had passed since I got that Bible as a gift.

I opened it and noticed that the teacher's aide had written a note on the front page with a Scripture reference of Proverbs 3:5-8. I turned to the reference and it read: "Trust in the Lord with all your heart, and lean not on your own understanding; in all your ways acknowledge Him, and He shall direct your paths. Do not be wise in your own eyes; fear the Lord and depart from evil. It will be health to your flesh, and strength to your bones." I just knew that God had given me that verse. He became very personal to me that day. He was speaking specifically to me right at that moment.

Over time, God not only healed my body, but He also began to heal the wounds inside me. For the first time in my life, I wasn't lonely. Then, the shame and guilt that I had carried throughout my life also dissipated.

Today I am married and have a family of my own. I am active at my church, and I am cancer-free. I spend my time reaching out to others that are suffering from emotional and physical pain, letting them know that God is real and wants to meet them in the midst of their circumstances and draw them near.

"Do not be wise in your own eyes;
Fear the LORD and depart form evil.
It will be health to your flesh,
And strength to your bones."
Proverbs 3:7-8

THINK ABOUT THIS

Obviously Craig's death had nothing to do with Jeff's wish. Jeff was simply angry at the moment, but the timing was terrible. Already steeped in guilt and shame, Jeff was once again thrown into a situation that no boy is prepared to deal with. Jeff found his escape and relief in drugs, but only at the expense of everything else.

God can take the most hopeless situations and revive us to flourish beyond what we ever could have imagined. Nothing in this world can do that. Some may think that winning the lottery would do that for them, but that's not true. The revival is only temporary and, in most cases, ultimately destructive. Others believe fame would do it for them, but just pick up a magazine or newspaper and read about the unhappy and out-of-control lives of the rich and famous.

The Bible speaks about "... endurance inspired by hope in our Lord..." (1 Thessalonians 1:3). We must learn to trust God, surrender to Him, and then hang on. He will never leave us or forsake us and continuously seeks to restore every broken area of our lives in its proper time.

QUESTIONS WE SHOULD ASK

Do you have a "dusty old Bible" laying around your house? When was the last time you read it?

How has a poor self-image affected your life's decisions?

Can you list three ways in which you could reach out to God in the midst of your personal suffering?

Appendix . . .

Bible, Poor Self Image, Suffering

twenty-five

M A D D I E ' S   S T O R Y

An Endless Search

"Although this new boyfriend and I were sleeping together, he voiced no objection to it, even though his faith taught against sex outside of marriage."

I always longed to know my dad. My parents met in the Marine Corps and had an affair. Since my father was already married, he made a hasty departure when he found out my mom was pregnant, claiming I was not his child. My mom is black, my father is white, and I was always starved to fit in and belong somewhere, but I felt neither black nor white, so I didn't fit in anywhere.

I was raised Catholic and went to private Catholic schools most of my life. I had knowledge of, and even a belief in, God, but I was very turned off by religion. When I was in college, I joined ROTC, where I met my husband, Tom, who was an avid Pentecostal. Not only did his religion bring about a big change in my life, but it also became a major stumbling block in my belief in God. I saw so much hypocrisy. At church he was this incredibly holy man, but at home he was not a spiritual leader at all.

Right after college, I was commissioned as a second lieutenant in the United States Army and stationed in Germany. Tom went with me, but our marriage was already in trouble. I wasn't happy, and after only a year and half together, I wanted out. I read a book about reversing your lot in life and decided that what I needed was to get divorced. The book was actually about making money, but the message to me was about undoing a mistake I had made, which in this case was my marriage. I didn't feel my husband was treating me the way I thought he should. I was empty inside and made up my mind the marriage needed to end, especially since I was already developing another relationship with another man.

Tom wanted to go to counseling, which I reluctantly agreed to do. The counseling sessions didn't have a chance because I had already made up my mind to get out of the marriage. In a matter of months, I was divorced. I also ended my affair with the man I had been seeing, but immediately got involved with someone else.

The new man in my life was a Christian who encouraged me to read the Bible and attend Bible studies. He bought me a Bible and helped me to understand it. I struggled with the concept of Christianity because of the pretense I had seen in Tom. Although this new boyfriend and I were sleeping together, he voiced no objection to it, even though his faith taught against sex outside of marriage.

I broke up with him and pursued yet another relationship. It was a pattern that continued to build in my life. I was searching for fulfillment, acceptance, and security. I desperately wanted to be loved, but no man could fill the void I felt in my heart. Deep down, I still believed in God but decided to do my own thing. Drinking, partying, and men became my way of life.

When I returned to the United States, I decided it was time for a change. I left the Army and began pursuing a new career in acting. After some time and effort, I landed a job in Baltimore touring with a children's theatre group. I moved out of the apartment I was sharing with a male companion to start a new relationship with yet another man. I was excited about the prospects ahead, but something was still missing in my life.

One day I saw an ad in the paper for an educated athlete that sparked my interest, and I went on an interview for the job. It ended up being a multilevel marketing company. I really didn't know what that meant, but I liked the products, and it was something different to do.

After a year, I decided to pursue it full-time because of the potential for making a lot of money. I knew if I had more money, I would be happy, so I packed up all of my belongings, got in my car, and moved to Florida. However, just one month later, I was facing financial ruin. To help pay my mounting bills, I started waitressing.

I met this girl at work who was very kind and cheerful. She seemed so different. She invited me to go to church with her, something I was not interested in. I let her know I believed in God, but that I did not do the "church thing." And yet I was miserable. I was drinking heavily, and when I finally got kicked out of my apartment, I started to think about this friend and the "church thing."

I called and told her I would go to church with her on Easter. The church was too big, but the people were very kind. It was the first time I felt like I fit in... the first time I ever felt at home in a church.

After the church service, her mom invited me to live with them since they had an extra room. I accepted, moved in, and started going to church with them on a regular basis.

One Wednesday evening, I was struck by the pastor's message. It made me realize that I had been blaming other people's failures as an excuse to run away from God. The light came on. I had spent years running away from God, trying to fill the emptiness in my life with everything but God.

I got involved in Bible studies and began to grow in my relationship with God. I started reading the Bible on my own, too.

Before long, I left waitressing and got a job as a copy editor, and my endless stream of relationships ended.

Once all my meaningless relationships with men were out of the way, a longing to know my real father surfaced.

One afternoon, I was on the Internet when, just for kicks, I decided to type in my dad's name to see what would come up. To my surprise, his name appeared, with an address and phone number. I called right away. The phone rang and rang with no answer. I called again that evening and got an answering machine with a woman's voice. I quickly hung up. I prayed and called again early the next morning. A woman answered. "Can I speak to Mr. Tim Johnston?" I asked. "Who's calling?" she replied. I gave my name. Soon I heard a man's voice say, "Hello?" I told him that, although he didn't know me, I believed he knew my mom. I asked if he had been in the Marine Corp. "Yes," he replied. I asked if he knew a Penny Brock? Quietly... hesitantly...he replied, "Yes." I knew his wife was there, so I gave him my phone number and asked him to call when it was a good time. It wasn't long before my phone rang. Quickly grabbing the receiver, I heard his voice.

Nervously, I told him he was my father. We talked for more than an hour and had a good conversation. He acknowledged that he was my father, and we agreed to exchange pictures.

In one miraculous day came the answer to my prayers, the end of my search, and the beginning of a relationship with my father. I still have a relationship with him, but, more importantly, I have a relationship with my Heavenly Father. The emptiness inside me is gone because God has filled that void in my life with Himself.

> *"...if My people who are called by My name will humble themselves,*
> *and pray and seek My face, and turn from their wicked ways,*
> *then I will hear from heaven, and will forgive their sin*
> *and heal their land."*
> 2 Chronicles 7:14

THINK ABOUT THIS

What a vivid picture of our relationship with God! Maddie's greatest desire in life was to find her father, and all the while her Heavenly Father was there for her, and she didn't know it.

You would think a girl like Maddie would have found God along the way. She sure had enough experiences with people who claimed to have an understanding of Him, and yet, until she met Jesus all on her own and sought her own understanding of Him by reading the Bible, she was unable to fill the emptiness in her heart.

You see, it's about having your own personal relationship with God. You have to spend time talking to God and listening to Him through His Word. No one can know God through someone else. It's all or nothing with God. There are no acquaintances in heaven. He's your Father or He's not. If you haven't already, begin your search for God. He's there for you...

QUESTIONS WE SHOULD ASK

List the things in your life that pull you away from God.

How do you deal with your doubts about God?

In your search for God, do you know where to begin?

Appendix ...

Backsliding, Doubt, Jesus

twenty-six

R A F A E L ' S   S T O R Y

Letting Go

"Being religious seemed like a crutch to me. I didn't need anybody - I had built everything I had on my own efforts. As far as I was concerned, I was self-sufficient and self-motivated, and that was a good thing."

·

I grew up in San Salvador, the son of a wealthy family. I had everything I needed and more. Maids, gardeners, nannies, and cooks took care of the day-to-day tasks and duties around the family home. I never had to do anything, including hold down a job.

When I moved to Florida to go to college, I found my new life very challenging. I had to fend for myself and do things I wasn't used to doing. I stayed undisciplined, fell back on my self-assured, sanguine personality, and became the class clown.

I faced some serious problems in college because of my lack of concentration and poor study habits. To make matters worse, I hooked up with the "party" crowd and started smoking pot and getting involved with girls - something I had never done in San Salvador.

After two years of consistently bad grades, I switched my major from Marine Biology to Business, hoping to lighten my study load and have more time for fun and partying.

Although my parents paid for my college education and gave me an allowance, it was not enough to buy a car, so I got a summer job selling books door-to-door, and it turned into a very lucrative enterprise. The next fall when I returned to school, I showed up in a new car.

I had also discovered that I was a good salesman, so every summer I sold books. In fact, I was so good at it that the company sent me to different states to sell their products. I set up a little organization and had my friends selling books as well. The money started to roll in, and it seemed that I had found my niche.

By the time I finished college I was working full-time and making plenty of money.

I took a year off from school, and then, because my parents wanted me to, I started pursuing my MBA. Also, I had an ulterior motive - I wanted to be near my girlfriend, Angela.

Angela became my best friend and the love of my life. We had a wonderful relationship. I could tell her anything. We did everything together, and I knew that she was the one I wanted as my wife.

We got married right before my graduation from the MBA program. The first three years of our marriage were consumed with work. Angela worked as a nurse, and I worked in a job that demanded traveling three or four nights a week. This was a plus for us and for our marriage because when I came home, we would spend quality time sharing our thoughts and feelings.

After the birth of our first child, she decided not to go back to work.

I continued in my same job, acquiring more sales territory, which demanded more of my time.

Though my home life was good, my life on the road was a far different scene. I was lonely, and I turned to pornography to get me through. I did not know how dangerous and damaging it was.

Three months after our first child was born, Angela became pregnant again.

I got promoted to national sales manager for my company, which meant that I had to travel all the time. We moved from our small house into an apartment, hoping to find a bigger home. Five months into the pregnancy, Angela had a placenta previa condition, which put her pregnancy at risk. Our little boy was only five months old, and because of her condition, Angela had to stay in bed the entire last trimester.

While Angela struggled with her second pregnancy, I struggled with my new position. Although I was the youngest up and coming national manager the company ever employed, I did not do well. The pressure on me was overbearing. I was constantly frustrated, and I brought my frustrations home with me.

Angela was tired and frustrated herself. We agreed that she should spend the last two months of her pregnancy living with her mother so that she could get some help with our son and get some rest.

Meanwhile, I went to work everyday fearing I would be fired.

After the birth of our second son, Angela moved back to our apartment. She was having a hard time handling two young children, and I was having my own troubles handling my job, so I didn't think much about what she was going through.

The pressure on our marriage was mounting.

Then the company I worked for was sold, giving me a reason to quit. A friend of ours, who made good money selling clothing items for another company, invited me to work with him. The money appealed to me, so I decided to give it a try.

The company's president and chairman were both Christian men. They had strong principles and ethics. Although I did not want to buy into the religious aspect of the company, I did like the men I worked for and the environment they created.

Being religious seemed like a crutch to me. I didn't need anybody - I had built everything I had on my own efforts. As far as I was concerned, I was self-sufficient and self-motivated, and that was a good thing.

When our sons were two and a half and one, Angela went back to work as an operating room nurse in Miami. She held a 7:00 a.m. to 3:30 p.m. shift, which seemed like it would work well with our family's schedule. This meant full-time daycare for the children - something that did not settle well with me.

When I went to Texas for two weeks of job training, Angela struggled with managing the children, getting ready for work, and trying to find full-time daycare.

Something happened during those two weeks. The pressure on her was more than she could take, and she basically had a nervous breakdown. Toward the end of the two weeks, she was screaming at the kids and totally out of control. I told her that it couldn't be that bad and, as a mom, she needed to figure out how to handle it.

I know now I was being self-centered, thinking only of my own job and my own worries. I was battling against feeling like a failure. That only magnified when I fell flat on my face in my new job.

Life at home was chaotic and escalating by the day. Both of us were exhausted and irritable. Angela's day started early. My day ended late. She would drop off the children at daycare around 6:30 a.m. and go to work in a high pressure and hectic operating room, only to pick up the children and arrive home at 4:30 p.m., just in time to make dinner for the family. I put in long hours trying to make sales calls and build relationships to boost my business.

Our marriage was in deep trouble. We became distant, isolated, and strained in each other's presence. The close friendship we had experienced in the beginning of our relationship was all but gone.

During this time I stepped up my pornographic use. I started craving more risque material, I became increasingly more dissatisfied with my wife, and we had very little intimacy together.

Then Angela informed me she wanted a divorce. I told one of my coworkers, who happened to be a former missionary, and he invited me to church. There he hooked us up with a counselor who told us the only thing that would save our marriage was for both of us to give our lives to Jesus Christ. I started to go to Bible studies. I began to read my Bible and pray, hoping for a change in our situation, but Angela had made up her mind to get a divorce.

I kept doing what I was doing, and a small but gradual change started to take place in my life. Three months later, Angela decided to give the marriage another chance. Our reconciliation lasted four months before tension filled the air worse than before, and she once again filed for divorce. I moved out of the house, and we divided up our personal belongings.

At this point, a secretary at my job told me about the church she went to and encouraged me to go. It was an evangelistic church that taught the Bible. I went, and I loved it. I gave my life to God there, and He met me right where I was, just like I was.

As for the divorce, I gave that to God as well. It was a rough time for us. We were going to mediation, but our negotiations had become bitter and messy. I still believed, despite all the turmoil, that God was in control, and that gave me peace.

While all this was going on, God blessed my business. I was

enjoying good sales and was once again making a living, but this time my life was consumed with God, not my job. I enrolled in the Bible college, and I spent every spare minute studying.

After our divorce was final, I determined not to date for at least a year. I totally devoted myself to God and the church. I got involved with teaching the children and was even picked to do an internship for the pastoral care ministry at my church.

Everything was going great except for one area of my life – Angela. I still resented her for leaving me, and every time I saw her, I got angry. When she started dating a doctor, my anger turned to despair.

Many people were praying that Angela would come to know God, and I was praying that God would help me get rid of the bitterness and resentment I felt toward her. God answered everyone's prayers.

Every Sunday I took my kids to church. One weekend the children invited their mother to come with us. She came, and after only two times, God touched her heart in such a mighty way that she surrendered her life to Him. Four years later, we got remarried. I thought I would never give up my sales job, but God had another plan for me. I became a children's minister at our church.

You know, when I tried to do everything my way, it would just become a tangled mess, but when I sought God first and did it His way and left my troubles in His hands, He brought my life and marriage back from the dead. God is faithful to His promises. He can do more than we could ever imagine.

> *"But seek first the kingdom of God and His righteousness,*
> *and all these things shall be added to you."*
> *Matthew 6:33*

THINK ABOUT THIS

The amazing thing about life is how easily it can get away from us. Rafael had started out with it all - wealth, comfort, family, friends, and all the trappings that for him translated into a life of leisure and very little responsibility, but he was missing something vital - character. His life was about himself, his life, his job, his schedule, his needs. That is where things began to go wrong.

What happens when your dreams turn to dust, and reality requires commitment and character? Success, and even survival, depend on what you are grounded in. In Rafael's case, because he lacked certain critical character traits, when heavy responsibility came his way, the easiest escape route came calling, and he followed after it. All of this resulted in a marriage that began to unravel. The fruit of a marriage that exists on the sole strength of each spouse results in a life of two people who just co-exist under the same roof. Rafael's wife needed him. She was not prepared to face child rearing alone. In his absence, they grew apart and lost that precious intimacy they had when their relationship first began.

Today, take a moment and evaluate where you have been, where you are, and where you are going. Rafael's life and marriage were saved when he observed the lives of a number of people who had a personal relationship with God. Who in your life can model that kind of relationship? Today his personal life, marriage, and career are fulfilling because of his relationship with God. He now has the privilege of building in the lives of young children something he did not have – a godly character based on a personal relationship with the Lord.

QUESTIONS WE SHOULD ASK

How would you describe your character traits? How would others describe them?

Is your security wrapped up in your finances? What things do you see as bringing you happiness?

Is there someone in your life you have observed that has a strong and vital relationship with God? Make a plan to go to that person and talk to him or her about God.

Appendix . . .

Self-Centeredness, Finances, Materialism

His Story

There is one more story, but it has yet to be written. That's your God story - that moment when you will encounter this life-changing, destiny-altering God who shows up at the most difficult times or at periods of quiet reflection, in the midst of madness or in the mire of the mundane. It is at these times when God softly and gently whispers your name and suddenly you become aware of a Presence that has always been there but that has been hidden by your many preoccupations with life.

Has something recently started to stir in your heart? It may be the very reason that you read this book, regardless of whether it was given to you by a friend or it just jumped out at you in a bookstore. But know this, you have just read one side of the story. There is another side, and that is God's Story. It's called the Bible. It is His Autobiography, written over a period of 1,600 years recording approximately 4,000 years of history, in three different languages, penned by 40 different authors living on three separate continents. The Bible contains 1,189 chapters, 31,173 verses, and 807,361 words. In it God has miraculously and painstakingly preserved His Story just for you. Were you to read it from cover to cover, do you know what you would find? You would find that God loves you, that He is madly in love with you, and that He wants to spend eternity with you. "For God so loved the world that he gave his only Son, so that everyone who believes in him will not perish but have eternal life" (John 3:16 NLT).

This is His Story:

It all begins in the book of Genesis. The essence of the story is simple and pure. God created man and woman, Adam and Eve, in His own image. He created them perfect and placed them in a perfect garden, which was on a perfect earth that was part of a perfect universe. God is quoted in Genesis as saying that everything He created was good – everything!

Part of God's wisdom in His creation of Adam and Eve was to provide them with a free will. He did not create puppets, but rather two people who were free to choose - to love and obey Him with all their heart, soul, mind, and strength, or to live life in a manner that was self-serving and independent of what God had planned for them. You may already know what happened next. Adam and Eve were deceived into believing that they could disobey God and get away with it, that they would become just like God if they did, and that God didn't really mean what He said anyway about eating that apple. Big mistake! The consequence was the Fall of Man - an eternal separation from God and banishment from the perfect Garden of Eden that He had created just for them. The consequence is actually quite logical. If God is holy and perfect and only makes perfect things, then once something becomes imperfect, He can no longer associate with it.

Adam and Eve's world began spiraling out of control. They faced hardships, disappointments, and pain they never knew existed. They experienced anger and fear, and there was no one to turn to but themselves. It didn't take long at all for the first murder to occur. Their first two sons fought, and eventually one killed the other out of jealousy. What was once a perfect existence was now imperfect and impure, and it was not due to any fault of God.

Thousands of years go by, and the matters of man deteriorate by the decade. Sin and evil abounded. Everyone did what seemed right in his own eyes. So God, being the loving, merciful Father that He is, devised a rescue plan to save His children from destroying themselves completely down here on earth.

As the story continues, the Bible takes us on an incredible journey of restoration. Yes, restoration. God's love for His world was so great that He was unwilling to let the situation continue as it was. Though everything was going to ruin, even to the extent that God was sorry He had even created man, He was still willing to pay the price of restoration. The price of restoration demanded His personal, human involvement in the situation. God did not delegate this; He couldn't and didn't want to. What a testimony of His love! The beloved (mankind) shunned the Lover, yet the Lover (God) was willing to pay any price to restore their relationship. This is the greatest story ever told. God loved us so much that He came to earth in human form to rescue us and redeem us from a destiny of destruction at our hands.

Easter celebrates God's redemptive act of restoration. Easter celebrates Jesus, who was God in the flesh, who came to earth to accomplish this very mission – to restore us to God. Jesus came to pay the price for every transgression, past, present, and future, that we have ever committed and would ever commit. He did this by going to the cross and dying in our place. His death paid our penalty, a sacrifice once and for all for every ungodliness of the human race. Our impurity is washed away through the ultimate sacrifice that Jesus made. The story of the cross, the tomb, and Christ's resurrection on the third day says it all: God loves you, God loves you, God loves you.

It has always been God's plan for you to belong to Him. He created you to love you, to walk through life with you, and to give you a future and a hope. Each God story in this book shares a common denominator. Each is a story of ordinary people who encountered the extraordinary love of God. Do you want to take a moment and let God record your encounter with Him right now in the chronicles of eternity?

The Bible speaks of a Book called the Lamb's Book of Life. Those who have had a life-changing encounter with God are recorded in this Book, which will be used to determine who enters Heaven and who does not: "Nothing impure will ever enter it, nor will anyone who does what is shameful or deceitful, but only those whose names are written in the Lamb's book of life" (Revelation 21:27 NIV).

If you are ready to have your God story written, then all you need to do is to acknowledge the Living God who is waiting to write His story on your heart. If you're wondering how to do that, it is as simple as talking to a friend. The Bible calls it prayer. Don't let the word "prayer" intimidate you. Prayer is not that inconsequential, sterile effort that you might remember from your religious upbringing. It is a form of communication in which you just tell God what is on your heart. As you let Him know that you realize how much He loves you and how you have been living your life without Him to no good end, the God talked about in this book will make His Presence known to you and restore your relationship with Him. He will take you out of the darkness in which you have been walking and bring you into the light of His goodness and kindness. He will gather up your life with all its broken pieces and replace it with His life - a life without end, a life everlasting. Then you, too, will have a God story to tell "written not with ink but by the Spirit of the living God, not on tablets of stone but on tablets of flesh, that is, of the heart" (2 Corinthians 3:3 NKJV).

If you are ready to receive the gift of eternal life, which was purchased for you by Jesus Christ at the cross of Calvary, then say to God, either out loud or in your heart:

God, I come to You with the faith of a child. I recognize that I am a sinner and in need of a Savior. I acknowledge that You came here to earth, in human form, to pay the penalty for my sins. I ask that You would forgive me and free me from the death sentence of sin by Your blood that was shed for me. I accept the gift of eternal life, which You purchased for me on the cross, where You suffered and died in my place. I believe You were buried and rose again on the third day. I ask that You would grant me, by Your grace,

through the faith You are giving me at this moment, salvation through Jesus Christ. Thank You, Father, for the gift of eternal life. Help me to live from this point forward in the grace that keeps me on the path of righteousness for Your name's sake. I ask these things in the name of Jesus. Amen.

Take a minute now and review the "next steps" that follow. They are the building blocks for your new life. Like every person you read about in this book, you, who were once far off, have been brought near to God. You are a new creation in Christ Jesus, created for God's glory and good works, which God has prepared beforehand just for you. Every angel in heaven rejoices that you have changed your heart and life! We can't wait to hear Your God Story!

THE NEXT STEPS
To Begin Your Walk with God

Talk Daily to God

Prayer is the biblical word for "talking" to God. Prayer is communication between you (a child of God) and your heavenly Father (God). Prayer does not have to be in the King James English for God to understand you ("Father, thou hast made me a blessed man.") No, God created you the way you are and He wants to spend time communicating with you. Go ahead; thank Him for the beautiful day. Ask Him for guidance in the difficult circumstance you are in. Most important of all, ask Him to give you strength and wisdom to live a life that is pleasing to Him. As you open your Bible to read each day, ask Jesus to open your eyes and your heart to see and hear what His Spirit will say to you.

SOME BIBLE VERSES TO READ
1 Thessalonians 5:17-18; Philippians 4:6-7; Psalm 34:1-8; Luke 18:1

Read the Bible

Get to Know God

The Bible says, "...as newborn babes, desire the pure milk of the word (the Bible), that you may grow." How would you feel if you had not eaten anything for three days? You would feel like passing out! It is the same principle with spiritual nourishment. When you go for three days without reading the Bible and spending time with Jesus, you are spiritually starving. But, when you spend time each day with Jesus, you will be spiritually satisfied. Ask yourself each night before you close your eyes to sleep, "Did I learn something new about Jesus today? What promise did Jesus reveal to me today? How have I become more like Jesus today?" If you cannot answer any one of these questions, don't close your eyes until you can. So, where do you start? If you don't have a Bible, go to a bookstore and buy one. Make sure it's one of those modern versions, written in plain English. With your Bible in hand, open up to the New Testament, (the second part of the Bible) and read about the life of Jesus. You can start by reading the book of John or the book of Luke. Take 15 minutes everyday and read one chapter or section until you are done. This will give you a good understanding of who Jesus was and is, what He said, what He did, and the basic principles of what it is to be a follower of Christ.

SOME BIBLE VERSES TO READ
2 Timothy 2:15; Psalm 1:1-3; Psalm 119:9-16; Ephesians 6:17; Hebrews 4:12

Go to Church

Spend Time with Believers

Fellowship is just a fancy word that simply means to hang around or interact with other Christians. To illustrate this, let's picture a barbecue with red glowing charcoal briquettes. If you reach in with tongs and take out one of those little briquettes and set it away from the others, what will happen to it? It will go out! It will get cold! Now, if you take that same briquette and place it back into the fire with the other briquettes, what will happen? It will once again take on the same characteristics of the other briquettes. And so it is with the Christian walk. If you surround yourself with other Christians and begin to share and pray together, you will not grow "cold" in your walk with Christ. So, make sure that you find a Bible-teaching, Bible-believing church, and find it soon. Next Sunday would be a good start! A Bible-teaching, Bible-believing church is a church that is known in its community for its good reputation, integrity, generosity (not hungry for money), friendly attitude, and ability to teach the Bible in a way that is always true and very applicable. Great music (worship) is important, too, because that is another way we get to know God. There...now it's up to you to start....

SOME BIBLE VERSES TO READ
Acts 2:42-47; Philippians 2:1-4; Ephesians 5:19-21; 1 John 1:5-7; Hebrews 10:24-25

Tell a Friend

Share Your Story with Someone

When you begin to live your life according to the first three principles above, you will be noticeably different. Those who know you will be able to see a change in your life. Witnessing, or sharing your faith, is just telling others what Jesus has done to bring about that change. Jesus says in the Bible, "Go into all the world and preach the Good News to all creation." Share what Jesus has done in your life. Find a friend, co-worker, family member, neighbor, or just a perfect stranger and tell that person what you have done. Talk about your "encounter with God." Do it soon, because it is a great way to make your decision all the more real. An added benefit to doing this is that you will be giving others the same opportunity you were given to live for God, right now, right here, and for all eternity with Jesus Christ in heaven.

SOME BIBLE VERSES TO READ
Acts 1:8; Matthew 5:14-16; Ephesians 6:19; Acts 4:13-21; Acts 10:42-43

N E W   B E L I E V E R, if you establish these four vital steps early in your Christian walk, you will become a strong follower of Jesus Christ, and you will experience your new Christian Life to the fullest. This will, without a doubt, be a decision you will never regret.

Just Let God Be In Control.

The Bible says that we are called by God "to love the LORD your God, to walk in all His ways, to keep His commandments, to hold fast to Him, and to serve Him with all your heart and all your soul."
- Joshua 22:5

A P P E N D I X

ABORTION
(value of children, forgiveness)

Psalm 139:13-16
For you created my inmost being; you knit me together in my mother's womb. {14} I praise you because I am fearfully and wonderfully made; your works are wonderful, I know that full well. {15} My frame was not hidden from you when I was made in the secret place. When I was woven together in the depths of the earth, {16} your eyes saw my unformed body. All the days ordained for me were written in your book before one of them came to be.

Romans 8:28
And we know that in all things God works for the good of those who love him, who have been called according to his purpose.

Psalm 42:11
Why are you downcast, O my soul? Why so disturbed within me? Put your hope in God, for I will yet praise him, my Savior and my God.

Psalm 103:8-12
The LORD is compassionate and gracious, slow to anger, abounding in love. {9} He will not always accuse, nor will he harbor his anger forever; {10} he does not treat us as our sins deserve or repay us according to our iniquities. {11} For as high as the heavens are above the earth, so great is his love for those who fear him; {12} as far as the east is from the west, so far has he removed our transgressions from us.

ABUSE
(the abused)

Psalm 34:4-5
I sought the LORD, and he answered me; he delivered me from all my fears. {5} Those who look to him are radiant; their faces are never covered with shame.

Proverbs 3:5-6
Trust in the LORD with all your heart and lean not on your own understanding; {6} in all your ways acknowledge him, and he will make your paths straight.

Isaiah 26:3-4
You will keep in perfect peace him whose mind is steadfast, because he trusts in you. {4} Trust in the LORD forever, for the LORD, the LORD, is the Rock eternal.

Matthew 11:28
Come to me, all you who are weary and burdened, and I will give you rest.

1 Peter 5:7
Cast all your anxiety on him because he cares for you.

2 Samuel 22:2-3
He said: "The LORD is my rock, my fortress and my deliverer; {3} my God is my rock, in whom I take refuge, my shield and the horn of my salvation. He is my stronghold, my refuge and my savior - from violent men you save me."

Isaiah 43:18
Forget the former things; do not dwell on the past.

Isaiah 54:4-6
"Do not be afraid; you will not suffer shame. Do not fear disgrace; you will not be humiliated. You will forget the shame of your youth and remember no more the reproach of your widowhood. {5} For your Maker is your husband - the LORD Almighty is his name - the Holy One of Israel is your Redeemer; he is called God of all the earth. {6} The LORD will call you back as if you were a wife deserted and distressed in spirit - a wife who married young, only to be rejected," says your God.

ADDICTIONS
(drugs, food, etc.)

Romans 6:2
By no means! We died to sin; how can we live in it any longer?

Romans 6:11-13
In the same way, count yourselves dead to sin but alive to God in Christ Jesus. {12} Therefore do not let sin reign in your mortal body so that you obey its evil desires. {13} Do not offer the parts of your body to sin, as instruments of wickedness, but rather offer yourselves to God, as those who have been brought from death to life; and offer the parts of your body to him as instruments of righteousness.

Romans 12:1
Therefore, I urge you, brothers, in view of God's mercy, to offer your bodies as living sacrifices, holy and pleasing to God - this is your spiritual act of worship.

Proverbs 5:22-23
The evil deeds of a wicked man ensnare him; the cords of his sin hold him fast. {23} He will die for lack of discipline, led astray by his own great folly.

Proverbs 23:20-21
Do not join those who drink too much wine or gorge themselves on meat, {21} for drunkards and gluttons become poor, and drowsiness clothes them in rags.

1 Corinthians 9:25-27
Everyone who competes in the games goes into strict training. They do it to get a crown that will not last; but we do it to get a crown that will last forever. {26} Therefore I do not run like a man running aimlessly; I do not fight like a man beating the air. {27} No, I beat my body and make it my slave so that after I have preached to others, I myself will not be disqualified for the prize.

ADULTERY
(the sin and forgiveness)

Matthew 15:19
For out of the heart come evil thoughts, murder, adultery, sexual immorality, theft, false testimony, slander.

Hebrews 13:4
Marriage should be honored by all, and the marriage bed kept pure, for God will judge the adulterer and all the sexually immoral.

1 John 1:9
If we confess our sins, he is faithful and just and will forgive us our sins and purify us from all unrighteousness.

1 Corinthians 7:3-4
The husband should fulfill his marital

duty to his wife, and likewise the wife to her husband. {4} The wife's body does not belong to her alone but also to her husband. In the same way, the husband's body does not belong to him alone but also to his wife.

Ephesians 5:3
But among you there must not be even a hint of sexual immorality, or of any kind of impurity, or of greed, because these are improper for God's holy people.

AFFAIR VICTIMS

1 Corinthians 13:4-5
Love is patient, love is kind. It does not envy, it does not boast, it is not proud. {5} It is not rude, it is not self-seeking, it is not easily angered, it keeps no record of wrongs.

Hebrews 12:15
See to it that no one misses the grace of God and that no bitter root grows up to cause trouble and defile many.

1 Peter 4:8
Above all, love each other deeply, because love covers over a multitude of sins.

1 Peter 5:7
Cast all your anxiety on him because he cares for you.

James 5:16
Therefore confess your sins to each other and pray for each other so that you may be healed. The prayer of a righteous man is powerful and effective.

Philippians 4:6
Do not be anxious about anything, but in everything, by prayer and petition, with thanksgiving, present your requests to God.

Psalm 34:18
The LORD is close to the brokenhearted and saves those who are crushed in spirit.

ALCOHOL ABUSE
(the sin and forgiveness)

Proverbs 20:1
Wine is a mocker and beer a brawler; whoever is led astray by them is not wise.

Proverbs 21:17
He who loves pleasure will become poor; whoever loves wine and oil will never be rich.

Proverbs 23:20-21
Do not join those who drink too much wine or gorge themselves on meat, {21} for drunkards and gluttons become poor, and drowsiness clothes them in rags.

Proverbs 23:29-32
Who has woe? Who has sorrow? Who has strife? Who has complaints? Who has needless bruises? Who has bloodshot eyes? {30} Those who linger over wine, who go to sample bowls of mixed wine. {31} Do not gaze at wine when it is red, when it sparkles in the cup, when it goes down smoothly! {32} In the end it bites like a snake and poisons like a viper.

Luke 21:34
Be careful, or your hearts will be weighed down with dissipation, drunkenness and the anxieties of life,

and that day will close on you unexpectedly like a trap.

ANGER
(controlling sinful anger)

James 1:19-20
My dear brothers, take note of this: Everyone should be quick to listen, slow to speak and slow to become angry, {20} for man's anger does not bring about the righteous life that God desires.

Proverbs 15:1
A gentle answer turns away wrath, but a harsh word stirs up anger.

Colossians 3:8
But now you must rid yourselves of all such things as these: anger, rage, malice, slander, and filthy language from your lips.

Proverbs 29:11
A fool gives full vent to his anger, but a wise man keeps himself under control.

Ephesians 4:31-32
Get rid of all bitterness, rage and anger, brawling and slander, along with every form of malice. {32} Be kind and compassionate to one another, forgiving each other, just as in Christ God forgave you.

not life more important than food, and the body more important than clothes? {26} Look at the birds of the air; they do not sow or reap or store away in barns, and yet your heavenly Father feeds them. Are you not much more valuable than they? {27} Who of you by worrying can add a single hour to his life?

Philippians 4:6-7
Do not be anxious about anything, but in everything, by prayer and petition, with thanksgiving, present your requests to God. {7} And the peace of God, which transcends all understanding, will guard your hearts and your minds in Christ Jesus.

1 Peter 5:6-7
Humble yourselves, therefore, under God's mighty hand, that he may lift you up in due time. {7} Cast all your anxiety on him because he cares for you.

Psalm 34:4
I sought the LORD, and he answered me; he delivered me from all my fears.

Psalm 37:7
Be still before the LORD and wait patiently for him; do not fret when men succeed in their ways, when they carry out their wicked schemes.

Proverbs 12:25
An anxious heart weighs a man down, but a kind word cheers him up.

ANXIETY, WORRY

Matthew 6:25-27
Therefore I tell you, do not worry about your life, what you will eat or drink; or about your body, what you will wear. Is

ASSURANCE OF SALVATION

John 3:16
For God so loved the world that he gave his one and only Son, that whoever believes in him shall not perish but have eternal life.

Job 19:25-27
I know that my Redeemer lives, and that in the end he will stand upon the earth. {26} And after my skin has been destroyed, yet in my flesh I will see God; {27} I myself will see him with my own eyes - I, and not another. How my heart yearns within me!

Romans 5:9-10
Since we have now been justified by his blood, how much more shall we be saved from God's wrath through him! {10} For if, when we were God's enemies, we were reconciled to him through the death of his Son, how much more, having been reconciled, shall we be saved through his life!

Romans 8:16-17
The Spirit himself testifies with our spirit that we are God's children. {17} Now if we are children, then we are heirs - heirs of God and co-heirs with Christ, if indeed we share in his sufferings in order that we may also share in his glory.

Romans 8:38-39
For I am convinced that neither death nor life, neither angels nor demons, neither the present nor the future, nor any powers, {39} neither height nor depth, nor anything else in all creation, will be able to separate us from the love of God that is in Christ Jesus our Lord.

Romans 10:9-10
That if you confess with your mouth, "Jesus is Lord," and believe in your heart that God raised him from the dead, you will be saved. {10} For it is with your heart that you believe and are justified, and it is with your mouth that you confess and are saved.

1 John 1:9
If we confess our sins, he is faithful and just and will forgive us our sins and purify us from all unrighteousness.

BACKSLIDING

Hebrews 10:38
But my righteous one will live by faith. And if he shrinks back, I will not be pleased with him.

Hosea 14:4
I will heal their waywardness and love them freely, for my anger has turned away from them.

Jeremiah 2:19
"Your wickedness will punish you; your backsliding will rebuke you. Consider then and realize how evil and bitter it is for you when you forsake the LORD your God and have no awe of me," declares the Lord, the LORD Almighty.

Jeremiah 3:22
"Return, faithless people; I will cure you of backsliding." "Yes, we will come to you, for you are the LORD our God."

Galatians 6:9
Let us not become weary in doing good, for at the proper time we will reap a harvest if we do not give up.

1 John 1:6-7
If we claim to have fellowship with him yet walk in the darkness, we lie and do not live by the truth. {7} But if we walk in the light, as he is in the light, we have fellowship with one another, and the blood of Jesus, his Son, purifies us from all sin.

BAD HABITS

Philippians 4:13
I can do everything through him who gives me strength.

Psalm 119:11
I have hidden your word in my heart that I might not sin against you.

James 4:7-8
Submit yourselves, then, to God. Resist the devil, and he will flee from you. {8} Come near to God and he will come near to you. Wash your hands, you sinners, and purify your hearts, you double-minded.

Romans 6:11-14
In the same way, count yourselves dead to sin but alive to God in Christ Jesus. {12} Therefore do not let sin reign in your mortal body so that you obey its evil desires. {13} Do not offer the parts of your body to sin, as instruments of wickedness, but rather offer yourselves to God, as those who have been brought from death to life; and offer the parts of your body to him as instruments of righteousness. {14} For sin shall not be your master, because you are not under law, but under grace.

Luke 9:23
Then he said to them all: "If anyone would come after me, he must deny himself and take up his cross daily and follow me."

BIBLE, THE

2 Timothy 3:16-17
All Scripture is God-breathed and is useful for teaching, rebuking, correcting and training in righteousness, {17} so that the man of God may be thoroughly equipped for every good work.

2 Peter 1:20-21
Above all, you must understand that no prophecy of Scripture came about by the prophet's own interpretation. {21} For prophecy never had its origin in the will of man, but men spoke from God as they were carried along by the Holy Spirit.

Hebrews 4:12
For the word of God is living and active. Sharper than any double-edged sword, it penetrates even to dividing soul and spirit, joints and marrow; it judges the thoughts and attitudes of the heart.

Psalm 119:9
How can a young man keep his way pure? By living according to your word.

Psalm 119:105
Your word is a lamp to my feet and a light for my path.

BITTERNESS, HATE, RESENTMENT

Hebrews 12:14-15
Make every effort to live in peace with all men and to be holy; without holiness no one will see the Lord. {15} See to it that no one misses the grace of God and that no bitter root grows up to cause trouble and defile many.

Ephesians 4:31-32
Get rid of all bitterness, rage and anger, brawling and slander, along with every form of malice. {32} Be kind and compassionate to one another, forgiving each other, just as in Christ God forgave you.

Galatians 5:15
If you keep on biting and devouring each other, watch out or you will be destroyed by each other.

1 John 3:15
Anyone who hates his brother is a murderer, and you know that no murderer has eternal life in him.

1 John 4:20
If anyone says, "I love God," yet hates his brother, he is a liar. For anyone who does not love his brother, whom he has seen, cannot love God, whom he has not seen.

CHILDREN, CHILD ABUSE

Ephesians 6:4
Fathers, do not exasperate your children; instead, bring them up in the training and instruction of the Lord.

Colossians 3:21
Fathers, do not embitter your children, or they will become discouraged.

Proverbs 22:6
Train a child in the way he should go, and when he is old he will not turn from it.

Proverbs 29:17
Discipline your son, and he will give you peace; he will bring delight to your soul.

Psalm 127:3
Sons are a heritage from the LORD, children a reward from him.

Deuteronomy 6:6-7
These commandments that I give you today are to be upon your hearts. {7} Impress them on your children. Talk about them when you sit at home and when you walk along the road, when you lie down and when you get up.

CHURCH

Ephesians 4:3-6
Make every effort to keep the unity of the Spirit through the bond of peace. {4} There is one body and one Spirit?just as you were called to one hope when you were called? {5} one Lord, one faith, one baptism; {6} one God and Father of all, who is over all and through all and in all.

Romans 12:4-8
Just as each of us has one body with many members, and these members do not all have the same function, {5} so in Christ we who are many form one body, and each member belongs to all the others. {6} We have different gifts, according to the grace given us. If a man's gift is prophesying, let him use it in proportion to his faith. {7} If it is serving, let him serve; if it is teaching, let him teach; {8} if it is encouraging, let him encourage; if it is contributing to the needs of others, let him give generously; if it is leadership, let him govern diligently; if it is showing mercy, let him do it cheerfully.

1 Corinthians 1:10
I appeal to you, brothers, in the name of our Lord Jesus Christ, that all of you agree with one another so that there may be no divisions among you and that you may be perfectly united in mind and thought.

1 Corinthians 12:12-13
The body is a unit, though it is made up of many parts; and though all its parts

are many, they form one body. So it is with Christ. {13} For we were all baptized by one Spirit into one body - whether Jews or Greeks, slave or free - and we were all given the one Spirit to drink.

DEATH

Psalm 23:4
Even though I walk through the valley of the shadow of death, I will fear no evil, for you are with me; your rod and your staff, they comfort me.

John 10:27-28
My sheep listen to my voice; I know them, and they follow me. {28} I give them eternal life, and they shall never perish; no one can snatch them out of my hand.

John 14:1-3
Do not let your hearts be troubled. Trust in God; trust also in me. {2} In my Father's house are many rooms; if it were not so, I would have told you. I am going there to prepare a place for you. {3} And if I go and prepare a place for you, I will come back and take you to be with me that you also may be where I am.

Philippians 1:21
For to me, to live is Christ and to die is gain.

Philippians 3:20
But our citizenship is in heaven. And we eagerly await a Savior from there, the Lord Jesus Christ,

Psalm 116:15
Precious in the sight of the LORD is the death of his saints.

1 Thessalonians 4:14
We believe that Jesus died and rose again and so we believe that God will bring with Jesus those who have fallen asleep in him.

2 Corinthians 5:6-8
Therefore we are always confident and know that as long as we are at home in the body we are away from the Lord. {7} We live by faith, not by sight. {8} We are confident, I say, and would prefer to be away from the body and at home with the Lord.

DEPRESSION

Psalm 55:16-18
But I call to God, and the LORD saves me. {17} Evening, morning and noon I cry out in distress, and he hears my voice. {18} He ransoms me unharmed from the battle waged against me, even though many oppose me.

Psalm 16:7-8
I will praise the LORD, who counsels me; even at night my heart instructs me. {8} I have set the LORD always before me. Because he is at my right hand, I will not be shaken.

Psalm 42:11
Why are you downcast, O my soul? Why so disturbed within me? Put your hope in God, for I will yet praise him, my Savior and my God.

Psalm 73:26
My flesh and my heart may fail, but God is the strength of my heart and my portion forever.

Proverbs 3:5-6
Trust in the LORD with all your heart and lean not on your own understanding; {6} in all your ways acknowledge him, and he will make your paths straight.

Proverbs 18:14
A man's spirit sustains him in sickness, but a crushed spirit who can bear?

DISCOURAGEMENT

Psalm 55:22
Cast your cares on the LORD and he will sustain you; he will never let the righteous fall.

Matthew 5:11-12
Blessed are you when people insult you, persecute you and falsely say all kinds of evil against you because of me. {12} Rejoice and be glad, because great is your reward in heaven, for in the same way they persecuted the prophets who were before you.

Joshua 1:9
Have I not commanded you? Be strong and courageous. Do not be terrified; do not be discouraged, for the LORD your God will be with you wherever you go.

Deuteronomy 31:8
The LORD himself goes before you and will be with you; he will never leave you nor forsake you. Do not be afraid; do not be discouraged.

1 Peter 5:6-7
Humble yourselves, therefore, under God's mighty hand, that he may lift you up in due time. {7} Cast all your anxiety on him because he cares for you.

Philippians 3:13-14
Brothers, I do not consider myself yet to have taken hold of it. But one thing I do: Forgetting what is behind and straining toward what is ahead, {14} I press on toward the goal to win the prize for which God has called me heavenward in Christ Jesus.

DOUBT

Matthew 14:29-31
"Come," he said. Then Peter got down out of the boat, walked on the water and came toward Jesus. {30} But when he saw the wind, he was afraid and, beginning to sink, cried out, "Lord, save me!" {31} Immediately Jesus reached out his hand and caught him. "You of little faith," he said, "why did you doubt?"

John 14:1
Do not let your hearts be troubled. Trust in God; trust also in me.

John 20:29
Then Jesus told him, "Because you have seen me, you have believed; blessed are those who have not seen and yet have believed."

James 1:5-8
If any of you lacks wisdom, he should ask God, who gives generously to all without finding fault, and it will be given to him. {6} But when he asks, he must believe and not doubt, because he who doubts is like a wave of the sea, blown and tossed by the wind. {7} That man should not think he will receive anything from the Lord; {8} he is a double-minded man, unstable in all he does.

FAITH

Romans 10:17
Consequently, faith comes from hearing the message, and the message is heard through the word of Christ.

Hebrews 11:1
Now faith is being sure of what we hope for and certain of what we do not see.

Hebrews 11:6
And without faith it is impossible to please God, because anyone who comes to him must believe that he exists and that he rewards those who earnestly seek him.

Ephesians 2:8-9
For it is by grace you have been saved, through faith - and this not from yourselves, it is the gift of God - {9} not by works, so that no one can boast.

James 1:2-3
Consider it pure joy, my brothers, whenever you face trials of many kinds, {3} because you know that the testing of your faith develops perseverance.

1 Peter 1:6-7
In this you greatly rejoice, though now for a little while you may have had to suffer grief in all kinds of trials. {7} These have come so that your faith - of greater worth than gold, which perishes even though refined by fire - may be proved genuine and may result in praise, glory and honor when Jesus Christ is revealed.

Matthew 14:31
Immediately Jesus reached out his hand and caught him. "You of little faith," he said, "why did you doubt?"

Lamentations 3:22-24
Because of the Lord's great love we are not consumed, for his compassions never fail. {23} They are new every morning; great is your faithfulness. {24} I say to myself, "The LORD is my portion; therefore I will wait for him."

Isaiah 41:10
So do not fear, for I am with you; do not be dismayed, for I am your God. I will strengthen you and help you; I will uphold you with my righteous right hand.

FEAR

Isaiah 41:10
So do not fear, for I am with you; do not be dismayed, for I am your God. I will strengthen you and help you; I will uphold you with my righteous right hand.

Isaiah 43:1-2
But now, this is what the LORD says - he who created you, O Jacob, he who formed you, O Israel: "Fear not, for I have redeemed you; I have summoned you by name; you are mine. {2} When you pass through the waters, I will be with you; and when you pass through the rivers, they will not sweep over you. When you walk through the fire, you will not be burned; the flames will not set you ablaze.

Psalm 23:4
Even though I walk through the valley of the shadow of death, I will fear no evil, for you are with me; your rod and your staff, they comfort me.

Psalm 27:1
The LORD is my light and my salvation - whom shall I fear - The LORD is the

stronghold of my life?of whom shall I be afraid?

Psalm 34:4
I sought the LORD, and he answered me; he delivered me from all my fears.

Psalm 56:3-4
When I am afraid, I will trust in you. {4} In God, whose word I praise, in God I trust; I will not be afraid. What can mortal man do to me?

FINANCES

Deuteronomy 8:17-18
You may say to yourself, "My power and the strength of my hands have produced this wealth for me." {18} But remember the LORD your God, for it is he who gives you the ability to produce wealth, and so confirms his covenant, which he swore to your forefathers, as it is today.

Matthew 6:21
For where your treasure is, there your heart will be also.

1 Timothy 6:10
For the love of money is a root of all kinds of evil. Some people, eager for money, have wandered from the faith and pierced themselves with many griefs.

Malachi 3:10
"Bring the whole tithe into the storehouse, that there may be food in my house. Test me in this," says the LORD Almighty, "and see if I will not throw open the floodgates of heaven and pour out so much blessing that you will not have room enough for it."

Luke 12:15
Then he said to them, "Watch out! Be on your guard against all kinds of greed; a man's life does not consist in the abundance of his possessions."

Ecclesiastes 5:10
Whoever loves money never has money enough; whoever loves wealth is never satisfied with his income. This too is meaningless.

FORGIVENESS
(of others)

Matthew 6:14-15
For if you forgive men when they sin against you, your heavenly Father will also forgive you. {15} But if you do not forgive men their sins, your Father will not forgive your sins.

Matthew 18:21-22
Then Peter came to Jesus and asked, "Lord, how many times shall I forgive my brother when he sins against me? Up to seven times?" {22} Jesus answered, "I tell you, not seven times, but seventy-seven times."

Mark 11:25
And when you stand praying, if you hold anything against anyone, forgive him, so that your Father in heaven may forgive you your sins.

Luke 17:3-4
So watch yourselves. "If your brother sins, rebuke him, and if he repents, forgive him. {4} If he sins against you seven times in a day, and seven times comes back to you and says, 'I repent,' forgive him."

Ephesians 4:31-32
Get rid of all bitterness, rage and anger, brawling and slander, along with every form of malice. {32} Be kind and compassionate to one another, forgiving each other, just as in Christ God forgave you.

1 Peter 4:8
Above all, love each other deeply, because love covers over a multitude of sins.

GRIEF

Psalm 31:9-10
Be merciful to me, O LORD, for I am in distress; my eyes grow weak with sorrow, my soul and my body with grief. {10} My life is consumed by anguish and my years by groaning; my strength fails because of my affliction, and my bones grow weak.

Matthew 5:4
Blessed are those who mourn, for they will be comforted.

2 Corinthians 1:3-4
Praise be to the God and Father of our Lord Jesus Christ, the Father of compassion and the God of all comfort, {4} who comforts us in all our troubles, so that we can comfort those in any trouble with the comfort we ourselves have received from God.

Revelation 21:4
He will wipe every tear from their eyes. There will be no more death or mourning or crying or pain, for the old order of things has passed away.

Philippians 4:19
And my God will meet all your needs according to his glorious riches in Christ Jesus.

GUIDANCE

Proverbs 3:5-6
Trust in the LORD with all your heart and lean not on your own understanding; {6} in all your ways acknowledge him, and he will make your paths straight.

James 1:5-6
If any of you lacks wisdom, he should ask God, who gives generously to all without finding fault, and it will be given to him. {6} But when he asks, he must believe and not doubt, because he who doubts is like a wave of the sea, blown and tossed by the wind.

Deuteronomy 31:8
The LORD himself goes before you and will be with you; he will never leave you nor forsake you. Do not be afraid; do not be discouraged.

Psalm 25:9
He guides the humble in what is right and teaches them his way.

Psalm 32:8
I will instruct you and teach you in the way you should go; I will counsel you and watch over you.

Psalm 37:23
If the LORD delights in a man's way, he makes his steps firm;

GUILT

Romans 8:1-2
Therefore, there is now no condemnation for those who are in Christ Jesus, {2} because through Christ Jesus the law of the Spirit of life set me free from the law of sin and death.

1 John 1:9
If we confess our sins, he is faithful and just and will forgive us our sins and purify us from all unrighteousness.

John 8:36
So if the Son sets you free, you will be free indeed.

Isaiah 43:25
I, even I, am he who blots out your transgressions, for my own sake, and remembers your sins no more.

Isaiah 44:22
I have swept away your offenses like a cloud, your sins like the morning mist. Return to me, for I have redeemed you.

Isaiah 64:6
All of us have become like one who is unclean, and all our righteous acts are like filthy rags; we all shrivel up like a leaf, and like the wind our sins sweep us away.

Psalm 32:5
Then I acknowledged my sin to you and did not cover up my iniquity. I said, "I will confess my transgressions to the LORD"- and you forgave the guilt of my sin.

HEALING

James 5:13-16
Is any one of you in trouble? He should pray. Is anyone happy? Let him sing songs of praise. {14} Is any one of you sick? He should call the elders of the church to pray over him and anoint him with oil in the name of the Lord. {15} And the prayer offered in faith will make the sick person well; the Lord will raise him up. If he has sinned, he will be forgiven. {16} Therefore confess your sins to each other and pray for each other so that you may be healed. The prayer of a righteous man is powerful and effective.

2 Corinthians 12:7-9
To keep me from becoming conceited because of these surpassingly great revelations, there was given me a thorn in my flesh, a messenger of Satan, to torment me. {8} Three times I pleaded with the Lord to take it away from me. {9} But he said to me, "My grace is sufficient for you, for my power is made perfect in weakness." Therefore I will boast all the more gladly about my weaknesses, so that Christ's power may rest on me.

Psalm 103:2-3
Praise the LORD, O my soul, and forget not all his benefits - {3} who forgives all your sins and heals all your diseases,

Psalm 30:2
O LORD my God, I called to you for help and you healed me.

Psalm 34:19
A righteous man may have many troubles, but the LORD delivers him from them all;

Matthew 8:2-3
A man with leprosy came and knelt before him and said, "Lord, if you are willing, you can make me clean." {3}

Jesus reached out his hand and touched the man. "I am willing," he said. "Be clean!" Immediately he was cured of his leprosy.

HOMOSEXUALITY

Romans 1:24-27
Therefore God gave them over in the sinful desires of their hearts to sexual impurity for the degrading of their bodies with one another. {25} They exchanged the truth of God for a lie, and worshiped and served created things rather than the Creator - who is forever praised. Amen. {26} Because of this, God gave them over to shameful lusts. Even their women exchanged natural relations for unnatural ones. {27} In the same way the men also abandoned natural relations with women and were inflamed with lust for one another. Men committed indecent acts with other men, and received in themselves the due penalty for their perversion.

1 Corinthians 6:9-10
Do you not know that the wicked will not inherit the kingdom of God? Do not be deceived: Neither the sexually immoral nor idolaters nor adulterers nor male prostitutes nor homosexual offenders {10} nor thieves nor the greedy nor drunkards nor slanderers nor swindlers will inherit the kingdom of God.

1 Corinthians 10:13
No temptation has seized you except what is common to man. And God is faithful; he will not let you be tempted beyond what you can bear. But when you are tempted, he will also provide a way out so that you can stand up under it.

Leviticus 18:22
Do not lie with a man as one lies with a woman; that is detestable.

2 Corinthians 5:17
Therefore, if anyone is in Christ, he is a new creation; the old has gone, the new has come!

Ephesians 4:22-24
You were taught, with regard to your former way of life, to put off your old self, which is being corrupted by its deceitful desires; {23} to be made new in the attitude of your minds; {24} and to put on the new self, created to be like God in true righteousness and holiness.

HOPE

Psalm 146:5-6
Blessed is he whose help is the God of Jacob, whose hope is in the LORD his God, {6} the Maker of heaven and earth, the sea, and everything in them - the LORD, who remains faithful forever.

1 Thessalonians 1:3
We continually remember before our God and Father your work produced by faith, your labor prompted by love, and your endurance inspired by hope in our Lord Jesus Christ.

1 Peter 1:3
Praise be to the God and Father of our Lord Jesus Christ! In his great mercy he has given us new birth into a living hope through the resurrection of Jesus Christ from the dead,

Isaiah 40:28-31
Do you not know? Have you not heard? The LORD is the everlasting God, the

Creator of the ends of the earth. He will not grow tired or weary, and his understanding no one can fathom. {29} He gives strength to the weary and increases the power of the weak. {30} Even youths grow tired and weary, and young men stumble and fall; {31} but those who hope in the LORD will renew their strength. They will soar on wings like eagles; they will run and not grow weary, they will walk and not be faint.

Hebrews 10:23
Let us hold unswervingly to the hope we profess, for he who promised is faithful.

Romans 8:24-25
For in this hope we were saved. But hope that is seen is no hope at all. Who hopes for what he already has? {25} But if we hope for what we do not yet have, we wait for it patiently.

Romans 15:13
May the God of hope fill you with all joy and peace as you trust in him, so that you may overflow with hope by the power of the Holy Spirit.

Jeremiah 29:11
"For I know the plans I have for you," declares the LORD, "plans to prosper you and not to harm you, plans to give you hope and a future."

Psalm 147:11
The LORD delights in those who fear him, who put their hope in his unfailing love.

INFERIORITY

1 Corinthians 1:26-29
Brothers, think of what you were when you were called. Not many of you were wise by human standards; not many were influential; not many were of noble birth. {27} But God chose the foolish things of the world to shame the wise; God chose the weak things of the world to shame the strong. {28} He chose the lowly things of this world and the despised things - and the things that are not - to nullify the things that are, {29} so that no one may boast before him.

Galatians 1:10
Am I now trying to win the approval of men, or of God? Or am I trying to please men? If I were still trying to please men, I would not be a servant of Christ.

Psalm 8:3-5
When I consider your heavens, the work of your fingers, the moon and the stars, which you have set in place, {4} what is man that you are mindful of him, the son of man that you care for him? {5} You made him a little lower than the heavenly beings and crowned him with glory and honor.

Ephesians 2:10
For we are God's workmanship, created in Christ Jesus to do good works, which God prepared in advance for us to do.

INSECURITY

Psalm 16:8
I have set the LORD always before me. Because he is at my right hand, I will not be shaken.

Philippians 4:13
I can do everything through him who gives me strength.

2 Corinthians 3:4-5
Such confidence as this is ours through Christ before God. {5} Not that we are competent in ourselves to claim anything for ourselves, but our competence comes from God.

Hebrews 10:35-36
So do not throw away your confidence; it will be richly rewarded. {36} You need to persevere so that when you have done the will of God, you will receive what he has promised.

Romans 8:37
No, in all these things we are more than conquerors through him who loved us.

1 John 5:14-15
This is the confidence we have in approaching God: that if we ask anything according to his will, he hears us. {15} And if we know that he hears us?whatever we ask?we know that we have what we asked of him.

Zechariah 4:6
So he said to me, "This is the word of the LORD to Zerubbabel: 'Not by might nor by power, but by my Spirit,' says the LORD Almighty."

JESUS
(His death)

2 Corinthians 5:21
God made him who had no sin to be sin for us, so that in him we might become the righteousness of God.

Luke 23:44-47
It was now about the sixth hour, and darkness came over the whole land until the ninth hour, {45} for the sun stopped shining. And the curtain of the temple was torn in two. {46} Jesus called out with a loud voice, "Father , into your hands I commit my spirit." When he had said this, he breathed his last. {47} The centurion, seeing what had happened, praised God and said, "Surely this was a righteous man."

John 19:28-30
Later, knowing that all was now completed, and so that the Scripture would be fulfilled, Jesus said, "I am thirsty." {29} A jar of wine vinegar was there, so they soaked a sponge in it, put the sponge on a stalk of the hyssop plant, and lifted it to Jesus' lips. {30} When he had received the drink, Jesus said, "It is finished." With that, he bowed his head and gave up his spirit.

1 Peter 2:22-24
"He committed no sin, and no deceit was found in his mouth." {23} When they hurled their insults at him, he did not retaliate; when he suffered, he made no threats. Instead, he entrusted himself to him who judges justly. {24} He himself bore our sins in his body on the tree, so that we might die to sins and live for righteousness; by his wounds you have been healed.

Romans 5:6-8
You see, at just the right time, when we were still powerless, Christ died for the ungodly. {7} Very rarely will anyone die for a righteous man, though for a good man someone might possibly dare to die. {8} But God demonstrates his own love for us in this: while we were still sinners, Christ died for us.

1 John 2:2
He is the atoning sacrifice for our sins, and not only for ours but also for the sins

of the whole world.

LONELINESS

Matthew 11:28-30
Come to me, all you who are weary and burdened, and I will give you rest. {29} Take my yoke upon you and learn from me, for I am gentle and humble in heart, and you will find rest for your souls. {30} For my yoke is easy and my burden is light.

Isaiah 41:10
So do not fear, for I am with you; do not be dismayed, for I am your God. I will strengthen you and help you; I will uphold you with my righteous right hand.

Psalm 139:7-12
Where can I go from your Spirit? Where can I flee from your presence? {8} If I go up to the heavens, you are there; if I make my bed in the depths, you are there. {9} If I rise on the wings of the dawn, if I settle on the far side of the sea, {10} even there your hand will guide me, your right hand will hold me fast. {11} If I say, "Surely the darkness will hide me and the light become night around me," {12} even the darkness will not be dark to you; the night will shine like the day, for darkness is as light to you.

Joshua 1:9
Have I not commanded you? Be strong and courageous. Do not be terrified; do not be discouraged, for the LORD your God will be with you wherever you go.

Matthew 28:20b
And surely I am with you always, to the very end of the age.

John 14:23
Jesus replied, "If anyone loves me, he will obey my teaching. My Father will love him, and we will come to him and make our home with him."

LOVE OF GOD

John 3:16
For God so loved the world that he gave his one and only Son, that whoever believes in him shall not perish but have eternal life.

John 16:27
No, the Father himself loves you because you have loved me and have believed that I came from God.

Romans 5:8
But God demonstrates his own love for us in this: While we were still sinners, Christ died for us.

Romans 8:38-39
For I am convinced that neither death nor life, neither angels nor demons, neither the present nor the future, nor any powers, {39} neither height nor depth, nor anything else in all creation, will be able to separate us from the love of God that is in Christ Jesus our Lord.

Ephesians 3:17b-19
And I pray that you, being rooted and established in love, {18} may have power, together with all the saints, to grasp how wide and long and high and deep is the love of Christ, {19} and to know this love that surpasses knowledge - that you may be filled to the measure of all the fullness of God.

1 John 3:1
How great is the love the Father has lavished on us, that we should be called children of God! And that is what we are! The reason the world does not know us is that it did not know him.

1 John 3:16
This is how we know what love is: Jesus Christ laid down his life for us. And we ought to lay down our lives for our brothers.

1 John 4:10
This is love: not that we loved God, but that he loved us and sent his Son as an atoning sacrifice for our sins.

MARRIAGE

Genesis 2:18
The LORD God said, "It is not good for the man to be alone. I will make a helper suitable for him."

Genesis 2:24
For this reason a man will leave his father and mother and be united to his wife, and they will become one flesh.

1 Peter 3:7
Husbands, in the same way be considerate as you live with your wives, and treat them with respect as the weaker partner and as heirs with you of the gracious gift of life, so that nothing will hinder your prayers.

Ephesians 5:22-25
Wives, submit to your husbands as to the Lord. {23} For the husband is the head of the wife as Christ is the head of the church, his body, of which he is the Savior. {24} Now as the church submits to Christ, so also wives should submit to their husbands in everything. {25} Husbands, love your wives, just as Christ loved the church and gave himself up for her

Proverbs 31:10-11
A wife of noble character who can find? She is worth far more than rubies. {11} Her husband has full confidence in her and lacks nothing of value.

1 Corinthians 7:3-4
The husband should fulfill his marital duty to his wife, and likewise the wife to her husband. {4} The wife's body does not belong to her alone but also to her husband. In the same way, the husband's body does not belong to him alone but also to his wife.

MATERIALISM

Proverbs 23:4-5
Do not wear yourself out to get rich; have the wisdom to show restraint. {5} Cast but a glance at riches, and they are gone, for they will surely sprout wings and fly off to the sky like an eagle.

Ecclesiastes 5:10
Whoever loves money never has money enough; whoever loves wealth is never satisfied with his income. This too is meaningless.

Luke 12:15
Then he said to them, "Watch out! Be on your guard against all kinds of greed; a man's life does not consist in the abundance of his possessions."

1 Timothy 6:6-10
But godliness with contentment is great

gain. {7} For we brought nothing into the world, and we can take nothing out of it. {8} But if we have food and clothing, we will be content with that. {9} People who want to get rich fall into temptation and a trap and into many foolish and harmful desires that plunge men into ruin and destruction. {10} For the love of money is a root of all kinds of evil. Some people, eager for money, have wandered from the faith and pierced themselves with many griefs.

Hebrews 13:5
Keep your lives free from the love of money and be content with what you have, because God has said, "Never will I leave you; never will I forsake you."

1 John 2:15
Do not love the world or anything in the world. If anyone loves the world, the love of the Father is not in him.

OCCULT

1 Timothy 4:1
The Spirit clearly says that in later times some will abandon the faith and follow deceiving spirits and things taught by demons.

Ephesians 6:10-12
Finally, be strong in the Lord and in his mighty power. {11} Put on the full armor of God so that you can take your stand against the devil's schemes. {12} For our struggle is not against flesh and blood, but against the rulers, against the authorities, against the powers of this dark world and against the spiritual forces of evil in the heavenly realms.

Revelation 21:8
But the cowardly, the unbelieving, the vile, the murderers, the sexually immoral, those who practice magic arts, the idolaters and all liars-their place will be in the fiery lake of burning sulfur. This is the second death.

Leviticus 19:31
Do not turn to mediums or seek out spiritists, for you will be defiled by them. I am the LORD your God.

Isaiah 8:19
When men tell you to consult mediums and spiritists, who whisper and mutter, should not a people inquire of their God? Why consult the dead on behalf of the living?

PATIENCE, PERSEVERANCE

Psalm 37:7
Be still before the LORD and wait patiently for him; do not fret when men succeed in their ways, when they carry out their wicked schemes.

Psalm 40:1
I waited patiently for the LORD; he turned to me and heard my cry.

Philippians 4:11
I am not saying this because I am in need, for I have learned to be content whatever the circumstances.

James 1:2-4
Consider it pure joy, my brothers, whenever you face trials of many kinds, {3} because you know that the testing of your faith develops perseverance. {4} Perseverance must finish its work so that you may be mature and complete, not lacking anything.

Lamentations 3:25-27
The LORD is good to those whose hope is in him, to the one who seeks him; {26} it is good to wait quietly for the salvation of the LORD. {27} It is good for a man to bear the yoke while he is young.

Luke 9:23
Then he said to them all: "If anyone would come after me, he must deny himself and take up his cross daily and follow me."

POOR SELF-IMAGE

Psalm 8:4-5
What is man that you are mindful of him, the son of man that you care for him? {5} You made him a little lower than the heavenly beings and crowned him with glory and honor.

Philippians 4:13
I can do everything through him who gives me strength.

Genesis 1:26-27
Then God said, "Let us make man in our image, in our likeness, and let them rule over the fish of the sea and the birds of the air, over the livestock, over all the earth, and over all the creatures that move along the ground." {27} So God created man in his own image, in the image of God he created him; male and female he created them.

Philippians 2:5-8
Your attitude should be the same as that of Christ Jesus: {6} Who, being in very nature God, did not consider equality with God something to be grasped, {7} but made himself nothing, taking the very nature of a servant, being made in human likeness. {8} And being found in appearance as a man, he humbled himself and became obedient to death-even death on a cross!

PRAISE

Psalm 63:3-4
Because your love is better than life, my lips will glorify you. {4} I will praise you as long as I live, and in your name I will lift up my hands.

Psalm 96:4
For great is the LORD and most worthy of praise; he is to be feared above all gods.

Psalm 100:4
Enter his gates with thanksgiving and his courts with praise; give thanks to him and praise his name.

Isaiah 42:8
I am the LORD; that is my name! I will not give my glory to another or my praise to idols.

Isaiah 43:21
The people I formed for myself that they may proclaim my praise.

Hebrews 13:15
Through Jesus, therefore, let us continually offer to God a sacrifice of praise - the fruit of lips that confess his name.

PRAYER

Philippians 4:6-7
Do not be anxious about anything, but in everything, by prayer and petition, with thanksgiving, present your requests to God. {7} And the peace of God, which transcends all understanding, will guard your hearts and your minds in Christ Jesus.

James 1:6-8
But when he asks, he must believe and not doubt, because he who doubts is like a wave of the sea, blown and tossed by the wind. {7} That man should not think he will receive anything from the Lord; {8} he is a double-minded man, unstable in all he does.

Ephesians 6:18
And pray in the Spirit on all occasions with all kinds of prayers and requests. With this in mind, be alert and always keep on praying for all the saints.

Psalm 66:17-20
I cried out to him with my mouth; his praise was on my tongue. {18} If I had cherished sin in my heart, the Lord would not have listened; {19} but God has surely listened and heard my voice in prayer. {20} Praise be to God, who has not rejected my prayer or withheld his love from me!

1 John 5:14
This is the confidence we have in approaching God: that if we ask anything according to his will, he hears us.

Matthew 6:5-6
And when you pray, do not be like the hypocrites, for they love to pray standing in the synagogues and on the street corners to be seen by men. I tell you the truth, they have received their reward in full. {6} But when you pray, go into your room, close the door and pray to your Father, who is unseen. Then your Father, who sees what is done in secret, will reward you.

Jeremiah 29:12-13
Then you will call upon me and come and pray to me, and I will listen to you. {13} You will seek me and find me when you seek me with all your heart.

PRIDE

Proverbs 11:2
When pride comes, then comes disgrace, but with humility comes wisdom.

Proverbs 16:18
Pride goes before destruction, a haughty spirit before a fall.

Jeremiah 9:23-24
This is what the LORD says: "Let not the wise man boast of his wisdom or the strong man boast of his strength or the rich man boast of his riches, {24} but let him who boasts boast about this: that he understands and knows me, that I am the LORD, who exercises kindness, justice and righteousness on earth, for in these I delight," declares the LORD.

Matthew 20:26-27
Not so with you. Instead, whoever wants to become great among you must be your servant, {27} and whoever wants to be first must be your slave

Luke 14:11
For everyone who exalts himself will be humbled, and he who humbles himself will be exalted.

1 Corinthians 4:7
For who makes you different from anyone else? What do you have that you did not receive? And if you did receive it, why do you boast as though you did not?

1 Corinthians 10:12
So, if you think you are standing firm, be careful that you don't fall!

PROTECTION

Psalm 7:10
My shield is God Most High, who saves the upright in heart.

Psalm 34:7-8
The angel of the LORD encamps around those who fear him, and he delivers them. {8} Taste and see that the LORD is good; blessed is the man who takes refuge in him.

Psalm 91:9-11
If you make the Most High your dwelling - even the LORD, who is my refuge - {10} then no harm will befall you, no disaster will come near your tent. {11} For he will command his angels concerning you to guard you in all your ways;

Proverbs 3:24-26
When you lie down, you will not be afraid; when you lie down, your sleep will be sweet. {25} Have no fear of sudden disaster or of the ruin that overtakes the wicked, {26} for the LORD will be your confidence and will keep your foot from being snared.

Jeremiah 15:20-21
"I will make you a wall to this people, a fortified wall of bronze; they will fight against you but will not overcome you, for I am with you to rescue and save you," declares the LORD. {21} "I will save you from the hands of the wicked and redeem you from the grasp of the cruel."

Joshua 1:9
Have I not commanded you? Be strong and courageous. Do not be terrified; do not be discouraged, for the LORD your God will be with you wherever you go.

PROVIDENCE OF GOD

Isaiah 14:24
The LORD Almighty has sworn, "Surely, as I have planned, so it will be, and as I have purposed, so it will stand."

Isaiah 46:10
I make known the end from the beginning, from ancient times, what is still to come. I say: My purpose will stand, and I will do all that I please.

Ephesians 1:11
In him we were also chosen, having been predestined according to the plan of him who works out everything in conformity with the purpose of his will,

Psalm 103:19
The LORD has established his throne in heaven, and his kingdom rules over all.

Romans 8:28
And we know that in all things God works for the good of those who love him, who have been called according to his purpose.

Romans 11:36
For from him and through him and to him are all things. To him be the glory forever! Amen.

SALVATION

John 3:16
For God so loved the world that he gave his one and only Son, that whoever believes in him shall not perish but have eternal life.

Romans 3:23-24
For all have sinned and fall short of the glory of God, {24} and are justified freely by his grace through the redemption that came by Christ Jesus.

Romans 6:23
For the wages of sin is death, but the gift of God is eternal life in Christ Jesus our Lord.

Romans 10:9-10
That if you confess with your mouth, "Jesus is Lord," and believe in your heart that God raised him from the dead, you will be saved. {10} For it is with your heart that you believe and are justified, and it is with your mouth that you confess and are saved.

Ephesians 2:8-9
For it is by grace you have been saved, through faith - and this not from yourselves, it is the gift of God - {9} not by works, so that no one can boast.

1 John 1:9
If we confess our sins, he is faithful and just and will forgive us our sins and purify us from all unrighteousness.

Acts 4:12
Salvation is found in no one else, for there is no other name under heaven given to men by which we must be saved.

2 Peter 3:9
The Lord is not slow in keeping his promise, as some understand slowness. He is patient with you, not wanting anyone to perish, but everyone to come to repentance.

John 5:24
I tell you the truth, whoever hears my word and believes him who sent me has eternal life and will not be condemned; he has crossed over from death to life.

SEEKING GOD'S WILL

Romans 12:2
Do not conform any longer to the pattern of this world, but be transformed by the renewing of your mind. Then you will be able to test and approve what God's will is - his good, pleasing and perfect will.

Proverbs 3:5-6
Trust in the LORD with all your heart and lean not on your own understanding; {6} in all your ways acknowledge him, and he will make your paths straight.

James 1:5-6,22
If any of you lacks wisdom, he should ask God, who gives generously to all without finding fault, and it will be given to him. {6} But when he asks, he must believe and not doubt, because he who doubts is like a wave of the sea, blown and tossed by the wind. {22} Do not merely listen to the word, and so

deceive yourselves. Do what it says.

Psalm 37:4
Delight yourself in the LORD and he will give you the desires of your heart.

Psalm 37:23
If the LORD delights in a man's way, he makes his steps firm.

Psalm 32:8
I will instruct you and teach you in the way you should go; I will counsel you and watch over you.

Proverbs 16:9
In his heart a man plans his course, but the LORD determines his steps.

SELF-CENTEREDNESS

Luke 9:23-25
Then he said to them all: "If anyone would come after me, he must deny himself and take up his cross daily and follow me. {24} For whoever wants to save his life will lose it, but whoever loses his life for me will save it. {25} What good is it for a man to gain the whole world, and yet lose or forfeit his very self?"

Romans 12:3
For by the grace given me I say to every one of you: Do not think of yourself more highly than you ought, but rather think of yourself with sober judgment, in accordance with the measure of faith God has given you.

Romans 12:10
Be devoted to one another in brotherly love. Honor one another above yourselves.

James 3:14-16
But if you harbor bitter envy and selfish ambition in your hearts, do not boast about it or deny the truth. {15} Such "wisdom" does not come down from heaven but is earthly, unspiritual, of the devil. {16} For where you have envy and selfish ambition, there you find disorder and every evil practice.

Matthew 20:26-28
Not so with you. Instead, whoever wants to become great among you must be your servant, {27} and whoever wants to be first must be your slave - {28} just as the Son of Man did not come to be served, but to serve, and to give his life as a ransom for many.

1 Corinthians 10:24
Nobody should seek his own good, but the good of others.

SELF-CONTROL

1 Peter 1:13
Therefore, prepare your minds for action; be self-controlled; set your hope fully on the grace to be given you when Jesus Christ is revealed.

2 Peter 1:5-6
For this very reason, make every effort to add to your faith goodness; and to goodness, knowledge; {6} and to knowledge, self-control; and to self-control, perseverance; and to perseverance, godliness;

Titus 2:2-6
Teach the older men to be temperate, worthy of respect, self-controlled, and sound in faith, in love and in endurance. {3} Likewise, teach the older women to

be reverent in the way they live, not to be slanderers or addicted to much wine, but to teach what is good. {4} Then they can train the younger women to love their husbands and children, {5} to be self-controlled and pure, to be busy at home, to be kind, and to be subject to their husbands, so that no one will malign the word of God. {6} Similarly, encourage the young men to be self-controlled.

Proverbs 25:28
Like a city whose walls are broken down is a man who lacks self-control.

Proverbs 29:11
A fool gives full vent to his anger, but a wise man keeps himself under control.

SELF-PITY

Psalm 73:2-3
But as for me, my feet had almost slipped; I had nearly lost my foothold. {3} For I envied the arrogant when I saw the prosperity of the wicked.

Psalm 73:16-17
When I tried to understand all this, it was oppressive to me {17} till I entered the sanctuary of God; then I understood their final destiny.

Psalm 73:28
But as for me, it is good to be near God. I have made the Sovereign LORD my refuge; I will tell of all your deeds.

1 Kings 19:3-4
Elijah was afraid and ran for his life. When he came to Beersheba in Judah, he left his servant there, {4} while he himself went a day's journey into the desert. He came to a broom tree, sat down under it

and prayed that he might die. "I have had enough, LORD," he said. "Take my life; I am no better than my ancestors."

1 Kings 19:11-12
The LORD said, "Go out and stand on the mountain in the presence of the LORD, for the LORD is about to pass by." Then a great and powerful wind tore the mountains apart and shattered the rocks before the LORD, but the LORD was not in the wind. After the wind there was an earthquake, but the LORD was not in the earthquake. {12} After the earthquake came a fire, but the LORD was not in the fire. And after the fire came a gentle whisper.

Proverbs 15:13
A happy heart makes the face cheerful, but heartache crushes the spirit.

SEXUAL IMMORALITY

1 Corinthians 6:15-20
Do you not know that your bodies are members of Christ himself? Shall I then take the members of Christ and unite them with a prostitute? Never! {16} Do you not know that he who unites himself with a prostitute is one with her in body? For it is said, "The two will become one flesh." {17} But he who unites himself with the Lord is one with him in spirit. {18} Flee from sexual immorality. All other sins a man commits are outside his body, but he who sins sexually sins against his own body. {19} Do you not know that your body is a temple of the Holy Spirit, who is in you, whom you have received from God? You are not your own; {20} you were bought at a price. Therefore honor God with your body.

Colossians 3:5-7
Put to death, therefore, whatever belongs to your earthly nature: sexual immorality, impurity, lust, evil desires and greed, which is idolatry. {6} Because of these, the wrath of God is coming. {7} You used to walk in these ways, in the life you once lived.

1 Thessalonians 4:3-5
It is God's will that you should be sanctified: that you should avoid sexual immorality; {4} that each of you should learn to control his own body in a way that is holy and honorable, {5} not in passionate lust like the heathen, who do not know God;

2 Timothy 2:22
Flee the evil desires of youth, and pursue righteousness, faith, love and peace, along with those who call on the Lord out of a pure heart.

1 John 2:15-16
Do not love the world or anything in the world. If anyone loves the world, the love of the Father is not in him. {16} For everything in the world - the cravings of sinful man, the lust of his eyes and the boasting of what he has and does - comes not from the Father but from the world.

SUFFERING

1 Peter 4:12-16
Dear friends, do not be surprised at the painful trial you are suffering, as though something strange were happening to you. {13} But rejoice that you participate in the sufferings of Christ, so that you may be overjoyed when his glory is revealed. {14} If you are insulted because of the name of Christ, you are blessed, for the Spirit of glory and of God rests on you. {15} If you suffer, it should not be as a murderer or thief or any other kind of criminal, or even as a meddler. {16} However, if you suffer as a Christian, do not be ashamed, but praise God that you bear that name.

2 Timothy 3:12
In fact, everyone who wants to live a godly life in Christ Jesus will be persecuted,

Romans 8:16-18
The Spirit himself testifies with our spirit that we are God's children. {17} Now if we are children, then we are heirs-heirs of God and co-heirs with Christ, if indeed we share in his sufferings in order that we may also share in his glory. {18} I consider that our present sufferings are not worth comparing with the glory that will be revealed in us.

Romans 5:3-5
Not only so, but we also rejoice in our sufferings, because we know that suffering produces perseverance; {4} perseverance, character; and character, hope. {5} And hope does not disappoint us, because God has poured out his love into our hearts by the Holy Spirit, whom he has given us.

2 Corinthians 12:7-9
To keep me from becoming conceited because of these surpassingly great revelations, there was given me a thorn in my flesh, a messenger of Satan, to torment me. {8} Three times I pleaded with the Lord to take it away from me. {9} But he said to me, "My grace is sufficient for you, for my power is made perfect in weakness." Therefore I will boast all the more gladly about my weaknesses, so that Christ's power may rest on me.

If you have enjoyed this book, and it has impacted your life, and you would like further teaching materials to strengthen your walk with God, we would like to hear from you.

Please contact us at:

Calvary Chapel Fort Lauderdale
2401 West Cypress Creek Road
Fort Lauderdale, Florida 33309

Or log on to www.myGodstory.com

We would also like to hear Your God Story. Contact us by e-mail at mystory@myGodstory.com.

DEVOTIONARY A Devotional With Meaning

This first publication by Pastor Bob Coy is a book of seventy-seven devotions. Its simple, dictionary-type format combined with biblical truths, real-life experiences, and light-hearted humor will bring new perspectives and deeper meaning to your daily time alone with the Lord.

the ACTIVE WORD CATALOG

If you would like additional resources (audio tapes, videos, CDs, and books) to help you grow in your knowledge of the Bible, please contact the Tape Ministry at Calvary Chapel Fort Lauderdale and request the Active Word Catalog at 1.866.222.9673 (toll-free) or by e-mail: tape@calvaryftl.org.